S0-BZY-884

ELECTRIC KILN CERAMICS

ELECTRIC KILN CERAMICS

SECOND EDITION

A GUIDE TO CLAYS AND GLAZES

RICHARD ZAKIN

CHILTON BOOK COMPANY

RADNOR, PENNSYLVANIA

A & C BLACK LONDON

Designed by Adrianne Onderdonk Dudden
Manufactured in the United States of America

Library of Congress Cataloging in Publication Data
Zakin, Richard.
     Electric kiln ceramics / Richard Zakin.—2nd ed.
        p.   cm.
     Includes index.
     ISBN 0-8019-8351-7
     1. Ceramics.   2. Electric kilns.   I. Title.
TP807.Z34   1993
738.1—dc20   93-30753
                                            CIP

1 2 3 4 5 6 7 8 9 0   2 1 0 9 8 7 6 5 4

CONTENTS

FOREWORD

There is a potter on one of the islands off the Vancouver coast who fires a whale-sized kiln with wood. Every time I meet him, it's shaking head time. How could anyone ever fire clay in one of those little, electric plug-in things? For him, no passage of fire, so no equation for quality. Maybe, too, sweat equity rules.

If there's enough heat to melt whatever fluxes are involved, you're in business. Sufficient melts can be achieved by firing with just peat, if that's what's needed. I've certainly done that; I've also fired higher by using the sun and a large, oil-filled lens. There have been different kinds of coal, coke, oil, and wood of all kinds in my life. And different kinds of gas—including a recent experiment that uses tap water and electricity to produce a potent hydrogen fuel by electrolysis. This latter process creates an intense, lance-like flame which can flow high-alumina firebrick to liquid within seconds. Only exotic as yet, and not much use except for iconoclasm, to me it represents peat's other end, as it were.

I like all kilns, the idea of kilns as heat containers, and not merely the rural lifestyle adjunct that goes along with some of them. It's true that I can't change an electrical atmosphere for long without paying the price. And it won't let me vapor glaze. But plug-in fuel, bourgeois and lifeless as it might be to others, readily brings me heat. I bring it fluxes. It's stable and convenient, available in most areas for the potter who repeatedly requires a predictable, clean atmosphere for certain other effects.

In fact, the only problem I actually have with electricity is its origin. Like the food return from grain-fed cows, to arrive at electricity from burning other sources seems redundant—a wasteful and dubious process. (I've read of it being a 1:1 return.) Only in hydro country does it make any sense; I'm grateful for that running water and those green hills far away.

It was twelve years ago that Zake's first book on electric kiln ceramics came out. A lot of curious and developing minds have passed through school since then; electric kilns have gotten somewhat better (although they still amazingly lack a protective collar device to safeguard the top bricks), and manufacturers of ceramic pigments have advertised wider palettes of color than ever before. As good as his first book looked when it came out, it appears somewhat skeletal in today's light. A new edition had to come along sooner or later and this one is most welcome in that it accommodates those changes. I'm especially glad that Richard has made expanded reference to special purpose clay bodies, brilliant glaze color and related underglazes, and richer surfaces from studio-made mixes. This new addition should confirm for the established, and suggest direction for the neophyte.

John Chalke
Calgary, Alberta
June, 1993

PREFACE

When I sat down to explain how I first took up oxidation firing, I found myself at a bit of a loss. I could dramatize and oversimplify the story, thereby turning myself into some sort of minor prophet, but I find the truth much more interesting. I know better than anyone that I took up my work with the electric kiln as a result of a mixture of accident, a vague understanding of my real needs, and helpful (if a bit perplexed) guidance from the faculty at Alfred University.

At the time I attended Alfred (1965–1967) reduction stoneware was still king, and we all learned how to work this way. These glazes were very beautiful, and I thought it unlikely that I would ever find glazes as stunning (I never have). As lovely as the reduction glazes were, however, they all had the same personality. The thick, complex glaze surfaces strongly dominated the form—took it over, in fact—softened it, and obscured it. I began to see that I needed simpler, leaner, glazes that did not necessarily obscure the body and any imagery I had created on its surface.

My reasons for moving to the electric kiln were quite simple and practical: I wanted to get colors and effects in my mid-fire and stoneware work which were unavailable to me with the fuel-burning, reduction kilns. To the surprise of everyone (especially me), even my first experiments with the electric kiln proved successful. The surfaces looked good on my work and allowed the body to show if I wished. They had two subtle advantages which I have come to value a greal deal: they were consistent and, even more important, they let me create complex, multilayer surfaces—indeed they required that I do so.

Many ceramists at that time, like me, were leaving high-fire reduction behind. However, while I was moving on to oxidation high-fire and mid-fire work, others, influenced by "Funk" ceramics from California, were moving to the brilliant color and painted surfaces of low-fire work. Most ceramists I knew thought I had gone in the wrong direction. At first it appeared that they might be right, but as time went on, it became apparent that there was indeed interest in electric-fired mid-fire and high-fire work.

Meanwhile I was beginning to get some good results, and I found that I really *liked* mid-fire and high-fire work in the electric kiln. In time, I developed acceptable glaze recipes and glaze application methods suitable for mid- and high-fire electric firing. I even began to lecture to craft groups about this kind of firing. The first time I did this was really an accident. I was giving a talk about my handbuilding techniques. Some people in the audience, on hearing that I was firing in an electric kiln, wanted to find out more about this aspect of my work. I began to do a little writing about my work with the electric kiln for the magazine *Ceramics Monthly*. At this time my good friend and colleague, the late Jean Delius encouraged me to write a book about the subject. The first edition of *Electric Kiln Ceramics* was published in 1981.

Though I still fire most of my work in the mid-fire, especially cone 3, I have come to like the low fire as well and work in it with some regularity. My change of mind is due in part to the way we think about ceramics at present. We have arrived at an interesting point in ceramics—one characterized by variety. Many ceramists are working in the high-fire range, mostly in fuel-burning kilns, but a significant number do their high-fire pieces in electric kilns. Many more ceramists are working in the mid-range, especially at cone 6. Most of this work is fired in the electric kiln, although some is fired in fuel-burning kilns. Many (especially those associated with colleges and universities) are working in the low fire, mostly in the electric kiln, but also in fuel-burning kilns (especially those who work in raku and also those who experiment with such methods as low-fire salt). Great work is being done in all these areas. I am glad that in this era there is more than one acceptable way to work. I prefer this polycentric environment; it is lively and always surprising.

In this complex environment I hope my book will take its place as an authoritative source of information on the ways the electric kiln can be used. I hope it will encourage ceramists to experiment in a host of ways with their imaginations running freely; for after all, isn't that why most of us took up work in the arts?

ACKNOWLEDGMENTS

No book of this sort can be called the work of one person: many people helped me in the creation of this book. I gratefully acknowledge their contributions.

My editor, Allison Dodge, had all the requisites of a good editor—patience, intelligence, and energy. I have enjoyed working with her on this book and the last (*Ceramics: Mastering the Craft*). Danielle Gordon made up glaze recipes and tested glazes, served as a reader, and kept track of correspondence and photographs. In other words, she handled much of the detail work that goes along with a project of this size. T. C. Eckersley took the technical photographs with his usual care and expertise. Mary Barringer suggested that I include material on the expenses incurred while running an electric kiln and sent me a good deal of useful material on this subject. David Gamble was the source of information and technical aid in the area of low-fire ceramics (with special emphasis on low-fire glazing). Ronald A. Kuchta, director of the Everson Museum of Art, has always been supportive of my work, and Michael Flanagan, the registrar, helped me with the photographs I needed for the historical section of this book. Finally I thank the many ceramists who have supported and encouraged me in my effort to deepen our understanding of appropriate methods for work in the electric kiln.

ELECTRIC KILN CERAMICS

INTRODUCTION

This book is intended for the potter who wishes to use the electric kiln to its fullest potential. Compared to fuel-burning kilns, the electric kiln is a recent invention, and we are still finding out how best to use it. When I wrote the first edition of this book in the late 1970s, many ceramists felt that electric kilns could not be used for serious work. Many thought of them as the "poor cousins" of fuel-burning kilns. Others thought that the electric kiln was fine for low-fire work but unsuited for the high fire. Perhaps the root of the problem lay in the fact that older recipes and techniques that worked beautifully with fuel-burning kilns tended to produce pallid, bland results in the electric fire. This was especially true of mid-fire and high-fire work.

In the ensuing years, however, the electric kiln's virtues of safety, convenience, and economy have made it extremely popular and encouraged its wide use. Now many ceramists understand how to use these kilns intelligently. For best results, the potter using the electric kiln should employ clay bodies and glazes formulated especially for the oxidation firing, which typifies this kiln. Ceramists indeed have had to develop a whole new spectrum of recipes and procedures to accommodate this firing. In the first edition of this book I developed a group of recipes and procedures tailored to the requirements of the electric fire. I have continued this process in this edition. It is my hope that this will help many ceramists to produce better work.

As electric kilns have come into wider use, ceramists have tried to understand oxidation firing practices of the past. The oxidation fire has been used by ceramists all over the world for a long time. It is well known that low-fire, lead-glazed ware was always fired in oxidation (this is because lead boils and blisters in reduction). What is not so well known is that mid-fire and high-fire oxidation work (in which lead was not used) created in the past was often of the very highest standard.

Now more electric kilns are used by contemporary ceramists than any other type. They are produced in large numbers and are sold at relatively low prices. Their economy, simplicity, and their relatively benign impact on the environment guarantee their great popularity. In addition, they lend themselves to a wide color range, are simple to load and fire, and are reliable and efficient. With the great popularity of the electric kiln has come a broad range of handsome, reliable clay-body and glaze recipes meant for the oxidation fire. These virtues are more than a convenience; they empower amateurs and professionals alike.

The electric kiln enables individuals with little access to support and training to work in clay when and where they wish. Many who would otherwise never be able to work in clay now can because of the electric kiln.

A whole new body of work in oxidation has been created since the first edition of this book was published more than a decade ago. This exciting work is, I feel, the real center point of this new edition of *Electric Kiln Ceramics*.

Note: In the first edition of this book I devoted considerable space to comparing the results of oxidation firing with that of reduction firing. At that time these comparisons were appropriate because reduction firing was the normative firing type. Now that this is no longer the case, I have decided to concentrate on useful and thorough descriptions of the way work looks after oxidation firing rather than comparing oxidation with reduction.

A DESCRIPTION OF THE ELECTRIC KILN

The electric kiln is a simple insulated box lined with coiled alloy wires that serve as a heat source (Fig. 1-1). The insulation allows heat to build up so that the ware can be fired. The walls of the kiln are made from soft, porous bricks that serve as the structural support of the kiln and also as its primary insulator. These bricks must be porous in order to be efficient insulators, but they must be strong enough to create a sound structure.

The coiled wires that line the sides of the kiln are called kiln elements; they are made from an alloy that can withstand high temperatures. The elements are placed into channels cut in the walls of the kiln. They are held in place in their channels with refractory metal pins to ensure that they will not come loose and sag during the stress of the high fire.

1-1. Contemporary high firing electric kiln.

Note the well-designed cable connection from one kiln ring to another. Cone Art Kilns from Tucker's Pottery Supply, Richmond Hill, Ontario. Sold in the United States by the Bailey Pottery Equipment Corp., Kingston, New York.

Each element is connected to a switch that controls the amount of current passing through it. A strong electric current passes through these tightly wound kiln elements and creates resistance; the elements become very hot (white hot in fact) and heat builds up inside the kiln. It is this heat, built up over time, that is used to fire the ware.

THE INFLUENCE OF THE OXIDATION ATMOSPHERE

The term "firing atmosphere" refers to the amount of oxygen inside the kiln chamber during firing. In the oxidizing fire, air is allowed free access to the firing chamber, and the atmosphere inside the chamber is well supplied with oxygen at all times.

While electric kilns can be constructed to allow for the creation of a reduction atmosphere (in which oxygen is restricted during the firing), most are not and electric kilns are generally fired in oxidation. The only exception to this is low-temperature saggar firing (see pp. 144). The even surface character of the piece fired in the electric kiln is far more compatible with the oxidation fire than with the reduction fire. On a more practical level, the life span of the alloys used in the kiln elements can be shortened if the atmosphere in the kiln chamber is reduced frequently.

The atmosphere inside an electric kiln is uniform and consistent, which encourages smooth and unbroken colors and visual textures.

Clay Bodies. Iron compounds in the clay body color it red, brown, or tan. Titanium compounds (common and influential clay body impurities) turn clay bodies ocher or gray-ocher. The firing encourages a smooth, unbroken body color, free of spots and uniform from the interior of the clay wall to its surface.

Glazes. Glaze color in oxidation is derived from colored glaze clays, naturally occurring colorants, and glaze stains. Colored glaze clays encourage earth reds, browns, soft greens, and ochers. The naturally occurring colorants encourage a broader color spectrum; tan, ocher yellow, brown, brick red, aqua, green, and blue. Glaze stains encourage the broadest color range (especially in the low fire) and include most of the colors available to artists in any medium, including the brightest oranges, yellows, burgundies, violets, and pinks.

Visual Textures. Visual textures tend to be smooth and unbroken in oxidation. However, a few materials (wood ash, lithium, and titanium) will encourage visual textures (as will calcium and magnesium in firings above cone 8). Furthermore, the application of one glaze over the other can strongly encourage visual texture, a condition that many oxidation-firing ceramists routinely take advantage of.

Glaze Surfaces. Glaze surfaces can be dry, mat, satin, smooth, or shiny. Most glazes for oxidation firing are simple and unbroken in their glaze surfaces; however, they are well adapted to complex glaze application and manipulation. The challenge for the oxidation potter is to give clay bodies and glazes a quality of richness and individual character. The ceramist can employ glaze materials and image-creation strategies that encourage a good deal of variety in surface, color, and visual texture.

PYROMETRIC CONES

Pyrometric cones are narrow three-sided pyramids used as indicators of the temperature inside the firing chamber. They are placed inside the kiln, in front of a spy hole bored through the wall of the kiln, and positioned in such a way as to be clearly visible during the firing. Made with many of the ingredients of clay bodies and glazes, pyrometric cones react not just to temperature but to a combination of time and temperature (often called "heat work"). As time passes and the temperature increases, the cones soften and bend. The ceramist uses the deformation of the cone as an indication that the clay bodies are mature, the glazes are melted and glassified, and that the firing is complete.

When ceramists speak of the conditions inside the kiln during firing, they often refer to a "cone," such as cone 04, or cone 3, or cone 6 because cones are the most accurate indicators of the conditions occurring inside the kiln during the firing.

FIRING TEMPERATURE

In this book I have chosen to work with five segments of the firing spectrum—cones 04, 02, 3, 6, and 9.

Cone	Nominal Temperature	
9	1280°C	2336°F
6	1222°C	2232°F
3	1168°C	2134°F
02	1120°C	2048°F
04	1060°C	1940°F

Note: Cones in the lower part of the firing spectrum have a zero in front of the number. The smaller the cone numbers after the zero, the higher the temperature. After cone 01, the zero is omitted and the cone numbers move from lower to higher, indicating hotter parts of the firing spectrum.

Cone 04 is at the lower end of the spectrum. Cone 02 is somewhat hotter but is still in the low-fire range. Cone 3 is in the middle of the firing spectrum. Cone 6 is hotter, but most ceramists still consider it to be a mid-fire rather than high-fire temperature. Cone 9 is at the high end of the firing spectrum. Each part of the firing range has its own unique character and each has its special value.

The Low Fire

Electric kilns are particularly suitable for low-fire work. They are especially efficient at low temperatures and encourage the use of brilliant color and strongly contrasting imagery.

Cone 04.   Cone 04 was originally associated with lead fluxes that melt (and melt beautifully) at low temperatures. Now that many ceramists no longer use lead (because it is toxic), we have found that cone 04 can be used with glaze recipes that contain powerful frits but are

1-2. Angelo di Petta. Toronto, Ontario. Bowls.

These pieces are made from a low-fire, white casting body. To create his surfaces di Petta brushes colorants, stains, and glazes on the piece. He fires to cone 06. In their complex imagery and brilliant color these bowls are very much representative of the low fire.

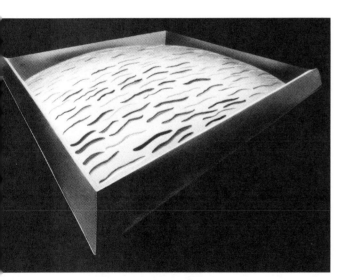

1-3. Ann Mortimer. New Market, Ontario, Canada. "Migration," 30 × 30 × 1.5 cm. Photo by Masao Abe.

Mortimer's pieces are made from a low-fire casting slip body. They are finished with glazes and "room temperature" highlights applied with a brush. Cone 04.

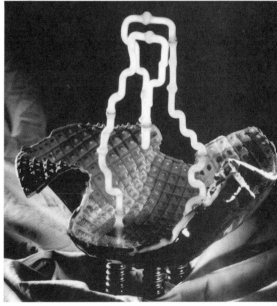

1-4. Rolando Giovannini. Faenza, Italy. "Neurotic Flower."

In this piece Giovannini effectively combines a low-fire formed tile piece with neon.

lead-free. While it is difficult to develop lead-free glazes that are stable and reliable at this part of the firing spectrum, it has proved to be possible.

Cone 02. This is the "high end" of the low fire. Many ceramists who work in the low fire without lead use this temperature for their work. Most, if not all, of the low-fire color range is still available here, and it is easy to develop stable and reliable glazes that contain sodium or boron frits but do not contain lead.

The Mid-Fire

Electric kilns are ideal for mid-fire work. They are efficient at these temperatures and encourage the use of strong color and durable and useful clay bodies.

Cone 3. Durable clay bodies and wide color range are powerful arguments for this part of the firing range; the potter has a wide choice of strong, saturated colors. At this temperature glaze recipes still must contain some frit but need not be dominated by these expensive materials. A strong argument in favor of cone 3 is economy; material costs can be kept low and firings are quick, inexpensive, and easy on the kiln.

Cone 6. Color still can be brilliant at cone 6 but not as brilliant as at the lower firing temperatures. Clay bodies are often very workable. A wide variety of clay-body types is possible; only true porcelain is not available at this temperature. Glazes need not be as strongly fluxed or carefully balanced as those intended for lower firing temperatures. The higher temperatures of cone 6 can be used to encourage rich visual textures.

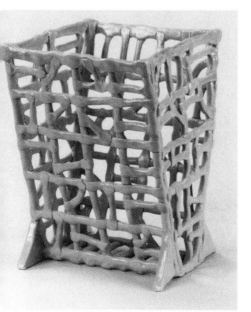

1-5. Richard Zakin. Oswego, New York. "Openwork Clay Basket," 22.3 × 17.5 × 16.5 cm. Photo by T. C. Eckersley.

In making this piece, I was inspired by the impromptu character of many low-fire pieces made in the past. Cone 02.

1-6. Richard Zakin. Oswego, New York. Vase, 15 × 19 cm. Photo by T. C. Eckersley.

I like the durable character and workable clay bodies of the mid-fire range and try to make pieces at this temperature that mirror these virtues.

1-7. Mary Barringer. Shelburne Falls, Massachusets. Untitled, 9 × 11 × 8 inches. Photo by Wayne Fleming.

Mary Barringer's light-colored stoneware pieces have a very strong high-fire identity. Cone 6.

The High Fire

Cone 9.   Color is more muted at the high-fire range than at the low and mid-fire. Clay bodies are workable and, when fired, durable. True porcelain is the province of cone 9 and above. Glazes are rich and reliable. At cone 9, fluxes such as calcium and magnesium come into their own and create the rich surfaces that this part of the temperature range is known for. Firing is time-consuming and is relatively expensive. Electric kilns are not quite as well suited for work at this part of the firing spectrum: elements used in cone 9 firings tend to become brittle far more quickly than those used only for firings at lower temperatures. At present, the manufacturers of elements for electric kilns recommend that they not be fired above cone 8 (1263°C/2305°F). However, if care is taken while glazing and cleaning, the longevity of the kiln elements will be preserved even if the kiln is fired often to cone 9 (1280°C/2336°F).

CLAYS AND CLAY BODIES

CLAYS

Clays are made up of crystalline structures that contain silica, alumina, and impurities. The character of clay has its strongly contradictory aspects. Though common, clay is a special material with unique properties. In itself it is formless, but it can be shaped into many forms. Although it is soft and pliable, it can be hardened by heat into one of the hardest materials known.

Clays are found throughout the world. Regardless of where they are found, they have the same basic makeup, and yet each deposit is unique. Though all are composed of silica, alumina, and impurities, they differ in the proportion of each material to the other and especially in the amount and types of the impurities they contain. They also vary in their particle size; some are comparatively coarse, while others are extremely fine.

CLAY BODIES

While we talk of working in clay, contemporary ceramists rarely work with a single clay: in truth, we work with "clay bodies." Clay bodies are mixtures of various clays and of nonclay materials. This is not a new development; early in the history of ceramics, potters learned how to modify the clays they found in nature by adding one clay to another or by adding nonclay materials, such as sand or wood ashes, to the clay. These potters were making the first clay bodies.

Both clay and nonclay materials are mixed together in a clay body to influence maturation temperature, color, particle size, shrinkage, and workability. Contemporary practice encourages working with clay bodies that are complex mixtures of materials from widely separated sources.

Recipes for clay bodies can be created for a particular purpose. I have taken advantage of that in this book to deal with clay body recipes that have been tailored to meet the needs of the ceramist working in the oxidizing fire of the electric kiln.

THE INFLUENCE OF THE OXIDATION FIRE ON CLAY BODIES
Surface

The surface of clay bodies fired in oxidation is uniform and unbroken. It is not marked by the strong firing reactions that can characterize work fired in a fuel-burning fire. This affects

2-1. George Mason. Newcastle, Maine. Wall piece, School Library, Biddeford Elementary School, Biddeford, Maine, 34 × 34 inches. Photo by Dennis Griggs.

Mason works almost entirely in the wall-piece format. He often uses an unglazed terra-cotta clay body, as he has done in this piece. Mason works in the low fire (here cone 04).

body color, which tends to be neutral and sober, and the visual texture of the clay surface, which is usually smooth and uniform.

Color and Character

In the low fire, the color of low-fire light-colored clay bodies is ivory or buff. These bodies are neutral in character and do not darken the color of glazes applied over them. Darker bodies may vary from ocher to brick red "terra-cotta" (a popular type) to deep brown. These can be rich in color and darken the color of glazes applied over them.

In the mid- and high fire, light-colored bodies can vary from cream white to light gray ocher. They are neutral in character but may slightly darken the color of glazes applied over them. Darker clay bodies will range in color from ochers, to dark tans, to browns and reds. These bodies can be rich in color and will strongly darken the color of glazes applied over them. Porcelain bodies are found only at the high fire. Color impurities are kept to a minimum: in the oxidation fire these bodies are white with a creamy tinge. Their character, while somewhat reticent, can be quite rich. Glazes applied over these bodies are particularly bright and lively in color.

Maturity

A clay body is said to be "mature" if it has been fired to a point where it is strong and dense but not fired to the point where it has become brittle. Maturity is reached in oxidation in the same way as in any other firing, and a body will be as mature if fired to a given firing temperature in oxidation as in reduction. There is, however, one important exception: bodies high in iron may mature more quickly in reduction than in oxidation. Because iron fired in reduction is more highly melted than iron in oxidation, the same body when fired in reduction will be somewhat more mature than when fired in an oxidation atmosphere.

Durability

Well-formulated and mixed clay bodies fired in oxidation are likely to be extremely durable and reliable.

2-2. Nino Caruso. Rome. ''The Memory Place,'' terra-cotta sculpture. Photo by Massimiliano Ruta.

Here and in Fig. 2-3 we see examples of architectural ceramics by the distinguished Italian ceramist Nino Caruso. In this figure the sculptural elements inside the room are finished with a white glaze and fired to 1280°C (cone 9 to 10).

CLAY-BODY TYPES

Low-Fire Clay Bodies

Because cone 04 is a low temperature, low-fire clay bodies require high percentages of strong fluxes. Strongly fluxed bodies of this sort are not tolerant of any overfiring; even localized hot spots can cause warping and glassification. Therefore, for safety's sake, low-fire

2-3. Nino Caruso. Rome. "Frame Doors." Large door, 11 × 7 feet; small door, 7 × 4 feet. Photo by Massimiliano Ruta.

Terra-cotta sculpture, fired in part to 1100°C (cone 02) and in part to 1280°C (cone 10). The architectural forms around the door are unglazed to highlight the character of the iron-rich terra-cotta clay body. They are cast-formed and fired to 1100°C (cone 02).

2-4. Sally Michener. West Vancouver, British Columbia, Canada. "Touch & Trace," 4 × 8 feet, wall piece, detail. Photo by Sally Michener.

In this tile installation Michener has combined commercial tiles and mirror fragments with unglazed terra-cotta elements. To achieve a broad spectrum of color the terra-cotta elements were fired at temperatures ranging from cone 010 to cone 01.

bodies should not be fired too close to maturity. The resulting immature bodies are not watertight or very dense. In general, however, they are reliable and easy to use.

Talc Bodies

Talc bodies are generally composed half of clay and half of talc. Their color is usually a pale ivory or buff. They do not darken the color of glazes applied over them.

Darker-Colored Low-Fire Bodies

The darker low-fire clay bodies rely in good part on iron compounds for both color and melting. They tend to contain large amounts of clay and in fact may be made from one to two clays with no other additions. Color varies from deep ocher to burnt orange to deep brown to red. These clay bodies strongly color any glazes applied over them.

Mid- and High-Fire Clay Bodies

Mid- and high-fire clay bodies do not require the strong fluxes appropriate to low-fire bodies. They can be fired to maturity and can be watertight, dense, and durable. In addition to being reliable, they are easy to use and highly workable.

2-5. Richard T. Notkin. Myrtle Point, Oregon. "Heart Teapot: Ironclad," Yixing Series, 6⅛ × 11⅝ × 4⅝ inches. Courtesy of the Garth Clark Gallery, New York and Los Angeles. Photo by R. Notkin.

In making unglazed work of this sort Notkin exploits the character of the stoneware body. Cone 5 to 6.

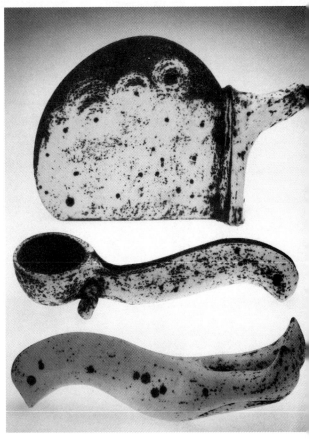

2-6. William Parry. Alfred Station, New York. "KFS–15," average length 15 inches. Photo by Brian Oglesbee.

Parry's work features rich surfaces; he often uses glazing strategies that partially reveal the clay body. Here he uses an intaglio technique for this purpose. Cone 6.

Stoneware Bodies

Stoneware clay bodies are composed mostly of clays and additions of 10 or 20 percent nonclay materials (often a feldspar and ground silica). The clays typically contain moderate amounts of impurities that darken and flux the body. Many stoneware bodies are somewhat coarse and may be considered "workhorse" clay body types. Grog or sand can be added to increase strength and provide a desired degree of coarseness. Most stoneware bodies are tan, gray, or brown.

Mid- and High-Fire Bodies with a Moderate Clay Content

Mid- and high-fire clay bodies may come close to stoneware in workability, but their identity is closer to low-clay bodies. They vary greatly in color, but common colors are off-whites, tans, soft grays, browns, and umbers. The sober and reserved character of these bodies is especially well suited to the oxidation fire.

Porcelain Bodies

While all clay bodies must adhere to a set of parameters, porcelain is the most strongly constrained by definite specifications. Porcelains must be white or cream or gray-white in

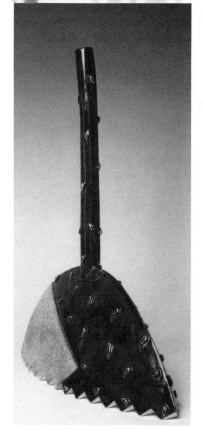
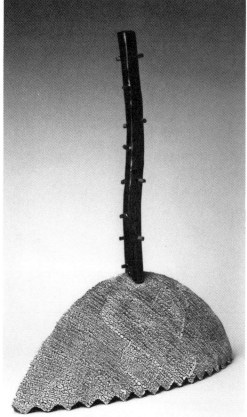

2-7. Richard Burkett. San Diego, California. LEFT: "Implement Vase," 17 × 16 × 4 inches. RIGHT: "Implement Vase," 18 × 16 × 4 inches. Photos by the artist.

In these two pieces Burkett uses a porcelain body fired to cone 6. The pieces are finished with cone 6 glazes and cone 06 overglazes. The dense white porcelain bodies heighten the glaze effect.

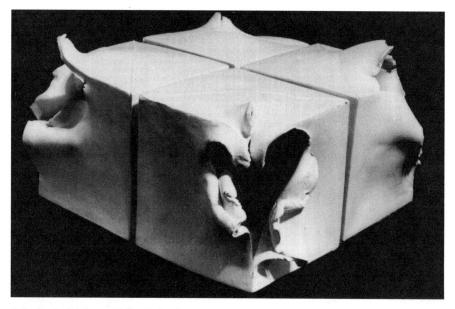

2-8. Ruska Valkova. Sofia, Bulgaria.

Valkova works in unglazed porcelain to emphasize the character of the body. The forms she chooses reveal the character of porcelain when it is manipulated.

color, their firing temperature must be cone 9 or higher, and the body must be translucent. Color and translucency must be achieved by using a formula composed of 45 percent or more nonplastic materials, namely, silica (flint) and flux (sodium or potassium feldspars only). The rest of the recipe is reserved for clay: though most definitions allow for some ball clay, most of the clay must be kaolin.

Porcelain bodies work especially well when fired in the oxidation atmosphere. The characteristics of the material and the fire match each other closely. Porcelain is a brilliant material and glazes look rich and vibrant over it. Many ceramic artists at the beginning of this century, such as Taxile Doat, Auguste Delaherche, and Adelaide Alsop Robineau, worked in oxidation-fired porcelain.

Because porcelains are high in nonclay materials, they are nonplastic and difficult to work with. These difficulties are compensated for by a uniquely refined character. Porcelain clay bodies are fine in texture and rich in body color and work well with glazes.

Porcelain is generally used for small- and medium-scale work in sculpture and pottery. Porcelain bodies do not have the plasticity and workability needed for large work. An experienced worker often will accept these risks, however, and push the limits of the material to work in a fairly large scale. Complex and highly personal methods may be devised for coping with the limitations of the material, including the addition of plasticizers and the use of special materials and specialized forming methods.

Porcelain-type Clay Bodies

If a clay body has some, but not all, of the characteristics of true porcelain (and the definition is narrow), it is usually called a porcelain-type clay body. The compromises that characterize these bodies will be suggested by a need for greater workability or a lower firing temperature. In practice, this may mean using a recipe that contains more clay than is allowed for in true porcelain, or a clay that contains impure clays or contains fluxes that limit translucency, such as dolomite.

Special-Purpose Clay Bodies

Along with the useful clay bodies listed above, there are many types of clay bodies made for specialized purposes. Unfortunately, these bodies are often restricted in their workability and stability. They can be exciting to work with, however, and educational as well, for they can teach the ceramist much about the nature of clays and clay bodies. From a large group of possibilities I have chosen to discuss a few types that are especially appropriate for the oxidation fire.

Translucent Low-Clay Bodies

These bodies generally contain 35 percent clay or less. Since clay is the source of workability in a clay body, these low-clay recipes are not particularly workable. They can be strikingly translucent and can be used to create unusual and evocative imagery.

Colored Clay Bodies

The color of clay is always appealing, and most ceramists experiment at one time or another with a colored clay or a group of colored clays. Colored clay techniques may be as simple as using the natural color of the clay body, or they may be more complex, requiring additions of clay-body stains. Clay-body stains are safer to use than normal coloring oxides, which are often toxic.

For polychrome colored clay techniques I prefer to use colored bodies with a low clay content similar to the translucent bodies discussed above. These bodies generally contain 35 percent clay or less. While they are not very workable, their low clay content helps the ceramist deal with the shrinkage and cracking problems that often mar colored bodies. Furthermore, they enhance stain color; it takes far less colorant to achieve a strong color in a low-clay body than in a body with the normal amount of clay.

Self-Glazing Clay Bodies

The appeal of self-glazing clay bodies is that they promise to eliminate the gap between the act of forming and the act of glazing. Self-glazing bodies contain water-soluble fluxes; as the piece dries, water migrates from its interior to the surface, where it evaporates. The water-soluble fluxes suspended in the water are deposited on the surface of the piece.

When the piece is fired, the fluxes combine with the silica and alumina in the body to create a thin layer of glaze on the surface of the ware. This self-glaze layer seems to emanate from the core of the piece and does not have the ''applied'' look that characterizes glazes.

An interesting variation on the self-glazing clay body is ''Egyptian paste.'' Egyptian paste bodies contain a soluble colorant (often one brilliant in color) as well as soluble fluxes. When carefully handled, these bodies allow the ceramist to blend color, surface, and form in a unique manner.

2-9. Vladimir Tsivin. St. Petersburg, Russia. Photo by Boris Smelov.

Tsivin uses grogged porcelain to create his figural pieces. Mostly he lets the clay speak for itself: this work is unadorned with surface finishes except for a few touches of glaze in some areas of the work.

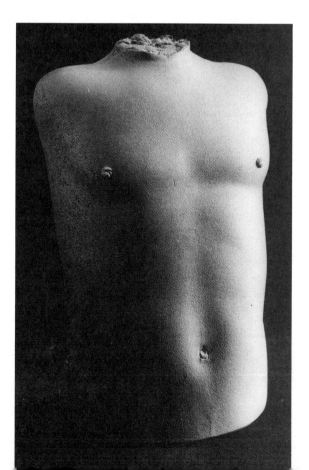

2-11. Barbara Frey. Commerce, Texas. "Round Trip Teapot #28," 7 × 9 × 4¼ inches. Photo by T. C. Eckersley.

Frey wedges body stains into a porcelain clay body, using slips and glazes for contrast. Cone 6.

2-10. Jennifer Lee. London. Dark pot with amber ellipse, emerging rim, 16 × 12 cm. Dark speckled pot with emerging rim, 15 × 12 cm.

Lee wedges oxides in the clay body (it is an uncolored, off-white stoneware). To enrich the surface and make it pleasant to hold, she need only sand the body with a fine sandpaper after it is fired. Cone 8 to 9.

2-12. Curtis and Susan Benzle. Hilliard, Ohio. "By Line," 7 × 7 × 4 inches. Photo by the artists.

The Benzles use a low-clay porcelain body with colorant and stain inlaid into the surface of the piece. Because this highly glassy body is liable to slump in the fire, it must be supported in a refractory form during firing.

2-13. Neil Forrest. Tantallon, Nova Scotia, Canada. LEFT: "Ornament with cathedral plan," 22 × 16 × 4 inches. RIGHT: "Diamond Panel," 28 × 18 × 4 inches. Photos by the artist.

In these pieces Forrest uses Egyptian paste clay bodies to create his tile backgrounds. These bodies are rich in surface and react strongly to color. Cone 010.

2-14. Gillian Lowndes. Bradfields, England. "Tea Strainers," 23 and 21 cm long.

These pieces are made from Egyptian paste, with mixed (metallic) media. They are fired to 1040°C. (Cone 05 to 04) (including their metal elements).

Unfortunately, the water-soluble melters necessary for self-glazing bodies interfere with the workable character of the clay and affect its stability; therefore self-glazing bodies tend to limit form possibilities and are difficult to work with.

Loaded Clay Bodies

Loaded clay bodies contain a high percentage of sand or grog. At such high percentages these additions not only control cracking and shrinking but also influence the look of the fired clay body. These clay bodies can be of great interest to the oxidation potter, for they are often soft yet stony in appearance. The addition of grogs and sands of various colors to clay bodies produces unusual visual textures. The ceramist will find these coarse-textured clay bodies appropriate for hand-formed work but unsuited for use on the potter's wheel, as they are abrasive.

COMMERCIALLY PREPARED CLAY BODIES

Most ceramists now buy their clay bodies already mixed and bagged from a commercial supplier. Most suppliers sell both a standard line of prepared clay bodies and customized clay-body mixtures. The mixing process demands specialized and expensive machinery. Furthermore, the process can be dangerous for the untrained person, so it often makes good sense to let professionals do the job.

A good supply house will pay great attention to detail to ensure that the clay bodies are reliable. Weighing, mixing, and cleaning must be carried out with rigorous care. The weighing of materials must be accurate and the mixing must be thorough. The mixing machinery must be cleaned between one clay body and another. Good suppliers make sure that these tedious and demanding tasks are done well and that no corners are cut. While price is a factor, the expense of the clay body is never large compared to the ceramist's investment of time and effort. The most important considerations in choosing a clay body supplier are support services and quality.

Choosing an Appropriate Clay Body

The appropriateness of a clay body depends on a number of factors:

1 The forming methods used

2 Firing temperature

3 Compatibility with the glazes chosen

4 The character and purpose of the pieces

Forming Methods.   Throwing bodies should be plastic and strong and resist collapse under the stress of throwing. They should not contain coarse materials or the thrower's hands will suffer. Hand-building bodies may be slightly less plastic but should be quite strong. They may contain coarse particles, which discourage warping and shrinkage and increase strength.

Firing Temperature.   Body and glaze must be compatible in firing temperature. The clay body must not mature at a point lower than the maturation point of the glazes. If it does, the body may melt or deform when the glazes are fired to maturity. Furthermore, the glazes should not mature at a point lower than the maturation point of the clay body. If this happens, the glazes will not fit the body: in this situation chipping will occur and most likely crazing as well. Some suppliers will label clay bodies as appropriate for a wide range of firing temperatures (for example, appropriate for cones 3 to 7). Clay bodies just do not work this way; they mature at a specific temperature and are best used at that temperature.

Compatibility with the Glazes Chosen.   Translucent and transparent glazes often do best when applied over light-colored bodies. If you use these glazes, consider changing the color of the clay body or use light-colored slips to mask the dark body. Carved imagery requires a body that contains no coarse particles. Delicate pieces suggest the use of fine-textured clay bodies, while less delicate work suggests the use of coarse clay bodies.

The Character and Purpose of the Pieces.   Utilitarian pieces (especially tableware) will require dense and highly durable bodies that are easily cleaned. The requirements for decorative pieces are not as exacting.

Standard and Custom Clay-Body Mixtures

Suppliers generally sell a standard line of prepared clay bodies, and they will probably suggest that you use one of these. These bodies are modest in price and are readily available. Most suppliers will also mix customized clay bodies (though they usually require that your clay body order be over a specified minimum weight, such as five hundred pounds or more). While custom clay bodies may cost more, they are more likely to fill your specific requirements.

Materials Substitutions

The availability of materials is a particular problem for both supplier and ceramist because the supply may be interrupted. Usually this interruption is temporary and of short duration, but occasionally it is permanent. A good supplier will notify you before making any substitutions. The supplier may feel that the substitution is in your best interest, but that decision should be left to you. When substitutions must be made, the supplier may be able to suggest a useful alternative.

Testing a Commercially Prepared Clay Body

Always check a new shipment of clay and make a few pieces or test tiles as soon as you take delivery. Fire the tiles and test them for absorbency. Though this process may at first sound daunting, a quick, fairly accurate body test can be performed in a matter of minutes. A more rigorous, scientific testing procedure will take longer but will be more reliable. See page 23 for clay body testing procedures.

Note: If you wish to ask your supplier to use any of the recipes in this book, feel free to do so.

TESTING CLAY BODIES

It is important that you know how to test clay bodies. These procedures are appropriate for testing clay bodies made in the studio and those produced by commercial suppliers.

Workability

Workability is a measure of the way the clay body can be manipulated. If you intend to create your forms on the potter's wheel, you will want a plastic and bendable clay body (and will be willing to put up with a good deal of shrinkage). If you intend to work with large, complex pieces, bendability will probably not matter so much. You will want a tough, durable clay body that has low shrinkage and is not prone to cracking.

To test for workability, roll out a coil of clay about one centimeter wide and 14 centimeters long. Bend it into the form of a script *e*. If it does not crack at the bend, it has a good deal of workability; if it does crack at the bend, workability is limited.

Absorption

One of the things you will most need to know about a clay body is its rate of absorption of moisture at your firing temperature. All fired clay bodies absorb some moisture; the rate of absorption can vary a good deal, however. I will discuss two procedures for testing for absorption. The first is an informal one that takes only a minute or two; the second takes more time but is far more accurate.

An Informal Clay-Body Absorption Test

Use a fired tile or even a fired piece; the base of a fired pot will do nicely if it is completely free of glaze. Apply a light coating of water on the testing area.

The object of the test is to observe the rate of absorption. If the water is absorbed into the clay body in a span of twenty to forty seconds, then the body is highly absorbent; if the water is absorbed in a span of two to three minutes, the body is only moderately absorbent. Absorption that takes longer than two or three minutes indicates that the body is mature. If the water stays on the surface of the clay without any absorption, it is possible that the body may have been overfired, in which case you should perform a simple slumping test (see below).

The Classical Clay-Body Absorption Test

Perform this procedure on a test tile made especially for the purpose. It should be fired to maturity and completely unglazed.

1 Take the test tile directly from the kiln as soon as it cools.

2 Weigh the tile (Fig. 2-15).

2-15. Weighing the test tile. Photo by T. C. Eckersley.

The tile will be immersed for 24 hours, then weighed again before the absorption rate is calculated.

3 Immerse the tile in water for twenty-four hours.

4 Remove the tile from the water and wipe away all surface water using a sponge and a tissue.

5 Weigh the tile again.

6 Subtract the original weight of the tile from the new weight (with absorbed water). The result is the weight of absorbed water.

7 Divide the old weight by the weight of absorbed water.

8 Move the decimal point two places to the right to get the absorption figure.

An Example of the Absorption Test

1 The weight of the tile as it is drawn from the kiln is 4.2 grams.

2 The weight of the tile after being immersed in water for twenty-four hours is 4.6 grams.

3 Subtract the original weight, 4.2 grams, from the weight after immersion, 4.6 grams. The weight of absorbed water is .4 grams.

4 Divide .4 by the original weight, 4.2 grams. This equals .095.

5 Move the decimal two places to the right: 9.5% is the absorption rate of the tile.

Appropriate Absorption Rates

While the absorption rate of a clay body is an objective measurement, judgment plays an important role: you must decide what sort of absorption rate is appropriate for your work. There is no one appropriate absorption rate for all clay bodies or for all types of ceramic work. If you work in porcelain, you will probably want a low absorption rate. If you are working in the low fire, you will probably not hold your clay bodies to such exacting standards.

The intended purpose of the work also plays an important part in judging the appropriate absorption rate. If you make utilitarian pieces, you may want a low absorption rate. However, if you are making sculptural or decorative pieces, a low absorption rate might not be appropriate. Below I list various clay body types and offer my judgment as to their appropriate absorption rate.

Clay-Body Type	Appropriate Absorption
Low fire	8 to 12%
Stoneware food containers	3 to 5%
Decorative stoneware	5 to 8%
Porcelain	1 to 3%
Sculpture bodies	10 to 20%

Clay-Body Shrinkage

Clay bodies shrink in both drying and firing. As is the case with absorption, appropriate shrinkage rates vary a great deal. No ceramist likes a high absorption rate, but if you are working with a fine-grained clay body with a low absorption rate such as a porcelain, you may have to accept a high rate of shrinkage as inevitable.

The Testing Procedure

1 Start with a sample of the clay recipe whose water content is typical of your normal clay bodies.

2 Make up a test tile 14 × 14 × .7 cm.

3 Draw a 10-cm line on the tile.

4 Let the tile dry and fire it to the desired temperature.

5 Measure the new length of the line.

6 Subtract the length of the line from 10 cm (the original length of the line).

7 Divide this figure by .10. This will convert the figure to a percentage of one hundred and will be the percentage of shrinkage.

Appropriate Rates of Shrinkage

As is the case with absorption, the intended purpose of the work also plays an important part in determining appropriate shrinkage rates. The ceramist who works with large pieces that cannot stand the strain of a high rate of shrinkage will have to work with coarse, highly absorptive bodies. If the ceramist working with a utilitarian piece decides that a low absorption rate is necessary, he or she may have to be willing to put up with a high shrinkage rate. Below I list various clay body types and give my judgment as to their appropriate shrinkage rate.

Clay Body Type	Appropriate Shrinkage
Low fire	8 to 12%
Stoneware food containers	12 to 15%
Decorative stoneware	10 to 14%
Porcelain	14 to 20%
Coarse bodies for large pieces	5 to 8%

Slumping and Warping

Slumping occurs when parts of the piece droop or sag in the fire. It is usually an indication of overfiring, and in most cases you will want to avoid it. Another sign of overfiring is a low absorption rate. If the clay body seems to have a low absorption rate and it slumps a great deal, this can be taken as proof that the body is overfired. Some slumping is to be expected, as much as half a centimeter, but if the clay warps more than that you will have difficulty firing the clay body to the temperature you wish to use.

Testing for Slumping and Warping

To test for slumping, support a test tile on each end and allow it to slump in the middle. The following procedure will help you obtain consistent results:

1 Make a test tile 16 cm long.

2 Let the tile dry completely.

3 Place refractory supports, one cm high, under each end of the tile (pieces of broken kiln shelf work well).

4 Fire the tile to the desired temperature (the tile need not be bisque-fired).

5 Measure the rate of slump. If it is more than half a centimeter, try another clay body.

CLAY BODY RECIPES

Cone 04 Clay Bodies

Classic Low-Fire Talc Body (50% clay, 50% nonclay)

talc	50		ball clay	50

This is the standard recipe for white-colored low-fire clay bodies. I have not yet been able to develop a recipe that works better than this one, which is fairly workable. When fired, its color and texture are acceptable. Like all cone 04 bodies, it is highly absorbent (nonabsorbent low-fire bodies will warp in the fire).

Long Point Red Body (50% clay, 50% nonclay)

soda spar	20		ball clay	25
talc	30		red clay	25

This clay body is especially appealing because of its rich salmon-pink color.

Cone 02 Clay Bodies

Taconic Dark Body (84% clay, 16% nonclay)

iron oxide	16		stoneware clay	12
ball clay	12		red clay	40
high-impurity clay	20			

This clay body is a red-brown color when fired to cone 02.

Orient Beach Buff Body (75% clay, 25% nonclay)

talc	25		fire clay	5
ball clay	35		stoneware clay	35

In color, this clay body is a light buff tan when fired to cone 02. It is quite workable.

Cone 3 Clay Bodies

Bowerstown Dark Fine Clay (85% clay, 15% nonclay)

talc	15	stoneware clay	25
ball clay	12	red clay	40
fire clay	8		

This strong and fairly workable clay body is a rich medium brown. This recipe appeared in the first edition of *Electric Kiln Ceramics.*

Taconic Dark Body (84% clay, 16% nonclay)

iron oxide	16	stoneware clay	12
ball clay	12	red clay	40
high-impurity clay	20		

This clay body is a rich mahogany brown when fired to cone 3.

Thacher Park Buff Body (50% clay, 50% nonclay)

talc	50	stoneware clay	25
ball clay	15	red clay	10

In color, this clay body is a rich, warm tan when fired to cone 3. It is quite workable.

Orient Beach Buff Body (75% clay, 25% nonclay)

talc	25	fire clay	5
ball clay	35	stoneware clay	35

In color, this clay body is a light, warm tan when fired to cone 3. It is moderately workable.

Cone 6 Clay Bodies

Cone 6 clay bodies offer the potter great advantages in terms of durability and workability. Only in the case of true porcelain is there any need to fire higher than cone 6. Cone 6 clay bodies can be made in a great variety of colors and tones, ranging from light off-whites to deep browns and umbers.

Stoneware Clay Bodies

The following three formulas are comprised of 90 percent clay and 10 percent nonclay materials.

Deep Red Stoneware Body (90% clay, 10% nonclay)

flint	10	ball clay	12
kaolin	33	red clay	45

This clay body is a deep brick red. It is not as strong or as easily worked as the salmon red body. Its color is quite rich. It is appropriate for small sculpture and hand-built pottery. This recipe appeared in the first edition of *Electric Kiln Ceramics.*

Orange Ocher Stoneware Body (90% clay, 10% nonclay)

flint	5	stoneware clay	70
potash feldspar	5	red clay	10
fire clay	10		

This clay body has a pleasing orange-ocher tone. It is a fine all-purpose clay body for pottery and sculpture. This recipe appeared in the first edition of *Electric Kiln Ceramics*.

Salmon Red Body (90% clay, 10% nonclay)

flint	5	ball clay	5
potash feldspar	5	stoneware clay	40
kaolin	20	red clay	25

This fine all-purpose clay body has a rich, medium-toned salmon color. It is smooth, plastic, easy to work with, and resistant to warping and cracking. This recipe appeared in the first edition of *Electric Kiln Ceramics*.

CHAPTER THREE

AN INTRODUCTION TO OXIDATION-FIRED SURFACES

We ceramists not only get a chance to work with clay and to make objects from it; we also have the opportunity to apply coatings, which act as finishes covering the surface of the piece. The ceramist can choose from a number of different surface finishes, each with unique advantages. Therefore it is important to know something about the behavior of each type of ceramic surface. In this chapter I will discuss various surface finishes useful to the ceramist working in the electric kiln.

In the second part of this chapter I will discuss color, an important aspect of surface finishes. Color is especially important to the ceramist working in the oxidation atmosphere of the electric kiln because rich, strong color is the hallmark of this firing atmosphere.

STAINED SURFACES

Stained surfaces are those to which thin washes of colorant, ceramic stain, or colored clays have been applied. The stains modify only the surface color, without covering or obscuring the clay body. Photos of pieces with stained surfaces begin on page 38.

The staining technique has three significant advantages:

1 The procedure is simple and reliable.

2 Stamped and carved images are shown to good advantage as a stained surface allows all clay textures to be clearly seen.

3 The stained surface is WYSIWYG (what you see is what you get). What you see before firing looks very much like the final product. This is important to ceramists who do not like the transformation that glazes undergo during firing.

Example: A Stained Surface

1 Imagery can be created on the surface of the piece while the piece is still in the green (unfired) state. You may use additive or subtractive methods to create the imagery. If you wish, fire the form to bisque.

2 Spray a thin solution of stain and water over the form. To create surface variations, spray more stain in one particular area.

3 Burnish the stain with a soft cloth.

4 The form is now ready for firing.

In a variation of this technique, the piece is first bisque-fired, then, with a sponge, a slip or a glaze is rubbed into the interstices of the form. This is cleaned so that the glaze remains only in the interstices (this is often called the intaglio method). The stain is now applied. Upon firing, the glazed areas will contrast nicely with those that are stained.

In another variation of this technique, a light or white glaze is sprayed over parts of the stained piece to contrast with the dark, mat surfaced stained areas.

TERRA SIGILLATAS

Terra sigillatas are mixtures of water and fine clay particles. When painted on clay, they produce a thin, waxy surface that is opaque, durable, and very beautiful. They are often fired in oxidation and do very well in the electric kiln. Photos of pieces made with terra sigillatas begin on page 44.

Making Terra Sigillatas

Terra sigillatas are essentially clay slips in which only the finest clay particles remain. To make a terra sigillata, clay is mixed with water and a deflocculant. Deflocculants are alkaline materials that break the bonds that hold clays together. The fine and coarse particles separate, and the coarse particles sink to the bottom of the container, from which they can be discarded. There are several methods used for collecting the fine particles: the siphoning method requires a wait of three or four days, after which the fine particles (which tend to gather in a layer in the middle of the container) are siphoned off. Another method (which I have used extensively) employs a decanting process: the mixture is passed from one container to another until all the coarse particles have been gathered and discarded. To ensure that no coarse particles remain in the terra sigillata, the ceramist can take the process one step further and grind the mixture in a ball mill (a machine for grinding liquids).

Here are directions for making a terra sigillata:

1 Choose a fine-particled clay such as a terra-cotta or a ball clay.

2 Mix the clay with water: use four times as much water (by weight) as clay. (If you do not use enough water, you will not get a good separation of the fine and the crude particles.)

3 Add the deflocculant sodium silicate (0.5% by weight [multiply by .005] for a red clay; 0.3% sodium silicate by weight [multiply by .003] for a white clay).

4 Stir the mixture thoroughly.

5 Pass the mixture through a sieve (30 mesh or finer).

6 In half an hour pour the slip from one container into another (wide-bottomed containers work best). When most of the slip has been poured out, you will see a coarse sediment at the bottom of the container.

7 Save the fine-particled clays and discard the coarse sediment.

8 Continue the process of pouring the slip back and forth between the two containers. Allow a short period of rest between each pour, about twenty minutes.

9 After 10 or 15 pours most of the coarse particles will be gone and the process is complete.

10 The mixture is very watery. Let it thicken by evaporation or simmer it (do not let it boil).

Occasionally (especially the first few times you try to make a terra sigillata), you may have difficulties with under- or over-deflocculated mixtures. If you have little sedimentation, you probably need more deflocculant; if you have *no* sedimentation, you probably have used too much deflocculant. Test the sigillata.

Testing the Terra Sigillata

Apply the sigillata to a test tile, and allow it to dry. Rub it lightly. If the sigillata is good, it will take on a perceptible shine and little, if any, of the sigillata will come off on your finger. If it is mat as it dries and it leaves a layer of clay on your finger, then it still contains too many coarse particles. Continue the decanting process or grind the mixture in a ball mill.

Problems with Terra Sigillatas

Terra sigillatas are difficult to make in part because the process is complex and somewhat unpredictable. It takes practice to make a mixture that contains only the fine particles. Even with practice the ceramist can expect surprises and setbacks. In my experience, those who are happiest with the process ball mill their terra sigillatas. Ball mills are bulky, noisy machines and are difficult to clean, but they can be relied on to produce a terra sigillata with a rich waxy surface.

Advantages of Terra Sigillatas

With all of these complexities and imponderables, it may seem surprising that anyone uses terra sigillatas at all. When terra sigillatas work well, however, they can be very appealing and create a beautiful surface. Their thin coatings do not obscure the clay body, and they can be used to produce a painterly imagery quite unlike any other ceramic surface.

How to Use Terra Sigillatas

Traditionally, terra sigillatas are finished in the low fire because only in the low fire will they take on their rich, soft sheen. If they are fired to higher temperatures, they will lose their sheen and take on a mat, stony look, although many ceramists find this effect appealing as well.

Terra sigillatas may be applied with a brush or a sprayer. Because they are clay slips, they flow very little and are WYSIWYG (what you see [before firing] is what you get [once the piece is fired]). They do, however, require some care in the application: they must be applied in thin layers or they will peel, blister, or flake.

Sgrafitto techniques require that the ceramist carve through a layer of slip or glaze to reveal the clay body. Terra sigillatas and sgrafitto imagery are often used together. The ceramist applies the sigillata to dry unfired ware and then carves through it to the clay body.

Terra sigillatas are most often used alone, but they may be combined with low-fire glazes.

SLIPS AND ENGOBES

Slips and engobes contain the same raw materials as glazes (clay, nonclay materials, and water). They differ only in their clay-to-nonclay ratios. Both are high in clay: slips contain 50 percent or more clay, and engobes contain 25 to 50 percent. These high clay amounts encourage dry surfaces (clays are refractory) that will not blur or run in the fire.

It is tempting to say that ceramic surfaces run or blur from the great heat inside the kiln, and it is true that many overfired surfaces run and blur even more than normal. But heat alone does not cause a glaze to run. Equally significant is the amount of alumina in the surface. A high-clay recipe, with its generous alumina content, will run and blur very little, if at all, for alumina imparts viscosity and stiffness to the formula. Because slips and engobes are high in alumina, they do not run.

Slips and engobes are compatible with other surface finishes and may be applied under glazes or used with stains. They are compatible with the oxidation fire because they encourage the creation of crisp graphic imagery.

Slips

Slips contain 50 to 100 percent clay. They are stable, durable, and will not run or blur in the fire. They may be applied when the clay is wet, dry, or bisque-fired. Slips applied to wet clay generally have a soft, natural character; slips applied to dry clay or to bisque-fired clay tend to have sharper edges and a precise, controlled character. Photos of pieces made with slips begin on page 53.

If you apply the slip to a wet clay body, use a normal (uncalcined) clay. If you apply it to dry or bisque-fired clay, most of the clay content should be calcined. To calcine clay, place it in a bisque-fired bowl and fire it to bisque. The clay will lose its water content and its plasticity; it will be dry, powdery, and nonshrinking. This last factor is important because it ensures a good fit between slips and dry or bisque-fired clay, both of which have already shrunk a great deal.

Gritty Slips

Slips usually are made from fine-grained clays and are sieved before they are used. The resulting texture is smooth and creamy. If some of the clays used in the recipe are coarse and the slip is not strained, the result will be a coarse, sandy-textured surface, which, although not practical for tableware (which must be easily cleaned), is appropriate for sculptural pieces.

Gritty slip recipes are simple mixtures of a few clays and perhaps a little flux. They may be applied by dipping, splashing, spraying, or brushing. If they are applied in a graphic, painterly manner, they will have characteristics similar to sand painting. Gritty slips may be applied to greenware or bisque-fired ware, and they may be used alone or in conjunction with stains and glazes. Gritty slips are reliable and easy to use. When fired, they are surprisingly strong and resistant to abrasion.

Engobes

Engobes have a clay content higher than glazes but lower than slips, varying from 25 to 50 percent. Engobes are best applied to dry greenware or to bisque-fired pieces. The nonclay additions can enhance durability, and a well-formulated engobe is likely to be somewhat more durable than most slips.

Vitreous Slips and Engobes

Vitreous means glass-like. We expect glazes to be vitreous, but we do not expect this of engobes, which have a high clay content. Although clay is refractory, engobes can be made vitreous if they are carefully formulated. This can be done by using strong fluxes in the recipe; these flux combinations are powerful enough to cause vitrification. Such recipes tend to be extremely stable and durable. They look and feel much like glazes (though they will generally lack any visual texture). Their high clay contents promote viscosity and they will not run or blur in the fire. It is thus possible to develop a technique that combines the richness and durability of glazes with the graphic, painterly qualities of engobes.

It is important to remember that many of these high-clay slips and engobes shrink a great deal. If they are applied to bisque-fired ware, much of their clay content should be calcined (see Slips, above).

Because of their greater durability, I prefer to work with engobes. Here are a number of recipes which I have found useful.

ENGOBE RECIPES FOR CONES 04, 02, 3, 6, AND 9

Six Corners Engobe 1   Cone 04

soda frit	48	zirconium opacifier	10
ball clay	30	titanium	2
Gerstley borate	10		

A variation of the Irelandville engobe listed below. This is a useful cone 04 engobe.

Irelandville Engobe 1   Cone 02

soda spar	38	Gerstley borate	10
soda frit	10	zirconium opacifier	10
ball clay	30	titanium	2

A useful durable engobe at cone 02.

Irelandville Engobe 2   Cone 02

soda spar	40	Gerstley borate	6
soda frit	10	zirconium opacifier	10
ball clay	32	titanium	2

Another useful durable engobe at cone 02.

Catchpole Engobe   Cone 3

soda spar	50	zirconium opacifier	10
ball clay	32	titanium	2
Gerstley borate	6		

A useful durable engobe for cone 3.

Thendara Engobe 1a   Cone 3

talc	28	opax	12
kaolin	46	borax	2
Gerstley borate	10	tin oxide	2

A stable and durable engobe with good color response. This is a variation of a recipe that appeared in the first edition of *Electric Kiln Ceramics.*

Ontario Engobe 1a   Cone 6

nepheline syenite	24	kaolin	36
flint	18	dolomite	10
boron frit	6	zircopax	6

A useful and reliable cone 6 engobe. This is a variation of a recipe that appeared in the first edition of *Electric Kiln Ceramics.*

Pilgrim Engobe 1a   Cone 9

potash feldspar	12	opax	12
talc	20	borax	2
kaolin	52	tin oxide	2

A strong cone 9 engobe. This is a variation of a recipe that appeared in the first edition of *Electric Kiln Ceramics.*

GLAZES

Glaze Surfaces

Glazes are a kind of glass, in many ways similar to common window glass. Glazes, however, are not meant to fit in a frame, as is window glass, but rather are meant to fit *over* a frame, that frame being the form of the clay object. Glazes are the most commonly used surface finish in ceramics and they offer the choice of a wide variety of visual effects—many of great beauty along with the virtues of durability and usefulness. Photos of a wide variety of glazed pieces begin on page 61.

Glaze Makeup

All glazes contain silica, alumina, and flux; in this respect they are the same as clay bodies. This similarity ensures that the bond between clay and glaze is very strong. The difference between the two is merely that glazes contain more flux and more powerfully melting fluxes than do clay bodies.

Glazes are formulated so that they become glass-like when fired to a desired cone or temperature range. They are carefully devised to bond well with clay and to color, decorate, and protect the form. Materials that modify glaze color (colorants), that render the glaze opaque (opacifiers), and that encourage strong visual textures may be added to the glaze to modify its appearance.

Glaze Character

Glazes take on many guises and vary a great deal in character. Because of these wide variations, it is helpful to group glazes into broad types or categories, determined by the following criteria:

Light Reflection.　They move from glassy and highly reflecting, to satin mat, mat or dry, and finally to stony.

Light Transmission.　They are transparent, translucent, or opaque.

Visual Texture.　They have no visual texture or are marked with visual textures to one degree or another.

Durability.　They are soft and easily scratched or are hard and durable.

Shiny, Mat, and Dry Surfaces

Potters use the terms shiny, smooth, satin, satin mat, mat, dry mat, and dry to indicate various types of glaze surfaces. Each surface type has its own character.

Shiny Glazes.　Shiny glazes convey a feeling of elegance and sophistication. They are used best on simple forms with smooth, unbroken surfaces. Shiny glazes strongly reflect light. They do not work well on complex, highly worked forms and surfaces, which can reflect the light in confusing patterns. In contrast, smooth, simple clay surfaces are enriched by the depth and luxurious character of shiny glazes.

Satin Mat Glazes.　Satin mat and mat opaque glazes have rich, soft surfaces, reminiscent of the soft surfaces of clay while it is being formed. Their clay-like character makes them valuable in sculpture and pottery.

Mat, Dry, or Stony Glazes.　These surfaces do not reflect much light; they are appropriate for highly manipulated forms, for which shiny glazes would be confusing. They tend to convey a rugged, rock-like feeling. Their pleasing character is not marked by the multiple reflections of shiny glazes; therefore they are suitable for use on complex forms and highly worked surfaces.

Light Transmission

Glazes vary in the way they transmit light. A transparent glaze transmits light clearly and efficiently. Translucent glazes are cloudy and transmit light less efficiently. Opaque glazes do not transmit light at all.

Transparent Glazes.   A transparent glaze is clear, transmitting light completely. Transparent glazes may be colorless or stained with color. Because well-formulated transparent glazes are among the strongest and most practical glaze types, they are often used on pieces intended for table use. In oxidation-fired ceramics, transparent glazes are especially luxurious when applied to white and porcelain bodies, for they dramatize the striking white color of the body.

Translucent Glazes.   Translucent glazes transmit light incompletely and partially reveal the character of the clay body. The cloudy surfaces of translucent glazes are especially appealing in that they can be softly modulated and offer a hint of the clay body underneath. Furthermore, they can pool and darken (especially if they are colored) where they are thick. They are especially rich over light-colored bodies. Translucent glazes are useful for both pottery and sculpture.

Opaque Glazes.   Opaque glazes transmit little or no light. While they do not reveal the character of the clay body, they can be quite rich and strongly marked with color or with visual texture.

Visual Texture

Though glazes can be completely free of visual texture (especially when fired in oxidation), the surface of many glazes exhibits a rich variety of these textures, including crystal patterns, light and dark modulations, pooling, and random flow. Glazes marked with visual textures are valued because of their rich, varied, and often surprising imagery. Many of these textures have a way of emphasizing manipulations on the surface of the clay body, an especially welcome characteristic. The addition of materials containing elements such as lithium, titanium, and zirconium encourages visual textures where they might otherwise not appear in glazes fired in an oxidation atmosphere. A number of the recipes in the next section have been formulated to encourage the formation of visual texture.

Utility and Durability

Glazes vary greatly in durability. Look for glazes that resist scratches and abrasions and are free from crazing, bubbling, and flaking.

For glazing utilitarian pieces, look for good durability and easy cleaning. You may want to use shiny or satin shiny glazes because they are easier to clean than glazes whose surface is mat or dry.

Many glaze materials that encourage rich character and visual textures also encourage soft, easily worn surfaces. The desire for a beautiful surface must be balanced against the need for durability. Ceramists who create nonutilitarian pieces tend to emphasize the look of the glaze, while those who create utilitarian pieces or work meant for outdoor sites will favor durable surfaces.

GLAZE COLOR IN OXIDATION

While glazes may be without color, just as window glass is without color, most ceramists use colored glazes. One of the most persuasive reasons for working with oxidation glazes is the availability of a broad spectrum of brilliant colors. Ceramic color must pass through the rigors of the kiln fire, where it takes on its fired color and its durable and unchanging character. The ceramist manipulates glaze color using colorants, stains, and colored clays.

Glaze Colorants

Colorants are materials that are used to impart color to ceramic surfaces. They are refined from minerals found in nature and added to the glaze in varying amounts, usually 0.5 to 4 percent of the total recipe.

The unfired color of the colorants is not always the same as the color that the colorants impart to the glaze when it is fired. This color change is one of the unpredictable aspects of glazing. In time the ceramist becomes familiar with the color changes that take place in the firing and learns to expect them, but even an experienced potter occasionally is surprised by the results of the glaze firing.

In the following I list the color each glaze colorant produces upon firing:

Clays: high-impurity clays will encourage creams, browns, rusts, and burnt oranges. Use up to 20 percent.

Cobalt: blue. Use up to 4 percent.

Copper: green. Use up to 4 percent.

Red iron oxide: earth yellow (with calcium), brown, soft yellow-green. Use up to 12 percent.

Black iron oxide: grays, browns. Use up to 12 percent.

Rutile: tans and browns. Use up to 2 percent.

A note on toxicity: Many colorants used in the past have proven to have toxic effects. At present, general practice substitutes glaze stains for these colorants.

Glaze Stains

Stains are made from naturally occurring ceramic colorants that have been modified by additions of oxides, which affect color. Oxides have created a whole new color palette for the ceramist. These colors are brilliant, safe to use, and very reliable. Stains are added to the glaze in varying amounts, usually 3 to 8 percent of the total recipe.

While these commercially produced stains are relatively expensive, they have certain advantages over naturally occurring colorants:

- Because they are fired in a very pure kaolin base and bonded with that base, they are safe to use.

- They are predictable and reliable.

- Their color is WYSIWYG (what you see is what you get).

Stains can be sensitive to their environment; their color will be heightened or diminished depending on the other materials in the recipe. In the first list typical glaze stain recipes are listed with their color. In the next list the glaze stains are listed with guidelines as to the kind of environment they need.

Chrome/tin-based—burgundy, pinks, and crimsons

Chrome/alumina-based—pinks and crimsons

Manganese/alumina—pinks

Alumina/chrome/iron compounds—browns and ambers

Titanium—yellow

Praseodymium—yellow

Vanadium/zirconium—greens and blue-greens

Chromium—greens

Cobalt/chrome/nickel/iron—grays and blacks

Following is the list of environmentally sensitive materials:

Burgundy, pinks, and crimsons (chrome/tin-based)—choose glazes that are high in calcium and tin, low in boron, and contain no zinc, titanium, or magnesium.

Pinks, crimsons (chrome/alumina-based)—choose glazes that are high in zinc, contain little calcium or boron, and contain no lithium.

Browns, ambers (chrome/iron-based)—choose glazes that are high in zinc and clay, low in tin, and with little calcium.

Yellow (titanium-based)—choose glazes that are low in calcium and tin.

Greens (chromium-based)—choose glazes that are high in calcium and contain no tin.

Grays and blacks (cobalt/chrome/nickel/iron)—choose glazes that do not contain titanium or zinc.

The following stains work well in any environment:

- Stains based on vanadium/zirconium—greens and blue-greens.

- Stains based on cobalt—blue, violet, gray, and black.

Note: The ceramist must be wary of the gases from chrome, cadmium, and vanadium during the firing because they are potentially dangerous.

Using High-Colored Clays in Glazes

While we use clays in glazes all of the time, we usually use clays that are white or cream in color. On many occasions, however, darker clays can be superior to light-colored clays in glazes. They can be especially useful in glazes intended for the oxidation fire. In my experience the most successful oxidation-fired earth-toned glazes derive their warmth from high-impurity clays rather than from the colorant iron oxide. While iron oxide seems to encourage neutral tones (greenish ochers and soft grass-green colors), impure clays encourage warm ivories, creams, earth oranges, reds, and browns. I value glazes that contain these clays because of their warm tones and rich visual textures.

In most areas it is easy to find an iron-rich clay for use in glazes. In North America we can use a widely distributed red clay: Cedar Heights Redart. While it is best known as a body clay, Redart is a fine glaze clay and I recommend its use. I have used Redart in glazes for many years and have found these glazes to be reliable, durable, and visually appealing. You will find that I use red clays in many recipes in this book.

You may also wish to use a darker colored, high-impurity clay in your glazes. I use a rich, dark clay called Barnard (widely available in North America), but similar red-brown, brown, and umber materials are found all over the globe. They too can encourage interesting and satisfying results.

STAINED SURFACES

Nancy Jurs. Scottsville, New York. LEFT: ''Still Life,'' 27 × 23 × 10 inches. Photo by Earl Kage. RIGHT: ''Still Life II,'' 24 × 20 × 7 inches. Photo by Lucy Horton.

Wall pieces. To attain a thin coating that does not obscure the clay body, Jurs sprays underglazes, oxides, and very thin coatings of glaze. These color the stoneware body without covering it. Cone 5.

Sue Abbrescia. Kalispell, Montana. TOP: ''Vessel #0258,'' 9 × 13½ inches. BELOW: ''Vessel #0232,'' 16 × 18 inches. Photos by Robert Sherwood.

Abbrescia wants to retain the coil details on the surface of her work. Therefore she stains her white earthenware clay bodies with thin coatings of slip and a cobalt oxide stain. Cone 5.

Mary Jane Edwards. Laramie, Wyoming. ABOVE: "Earth Container," 12 × 8 × 8 inches. OPPOSITE: "Earth Container," 13 × 7 × 7 inches.

Edwards brushes slips and oxides over a heavily grogged earthenware clay body. In this way she emphasizes the "rough, grainy surface texture" of the clay body. Cone 04.

Liliana Malta. Rome. TOP: ''Landscape Shadows,'' 18 inches high. BELOW: ''Archaic Trophy,'' 24 inches high. Photos by Massimiliano Ruta.

Liliana Malta applies thin washes of colorant oxide to a refractory clay body and fires this to 1100°C (cone 03).

Elizabeth MacDonald. Bridgewater, Connecticut. ABOVE: ''Sky,'' 40 × 40 inches. Photo by Eve Fuka. FAR LEFT: ''Box with Nest and Egg,'' 7 × 7 × 3 inches. LEFT: ''Box with Stairs,'' 13 × 6 × 2 inches. Photos by William Seitz.

While her stoneware clay is still wet, MacDonald presses ceramic stains into its surface, ''creating layers of color and a patina of age.'' Cone 6.

TERRA SIGILLATAS

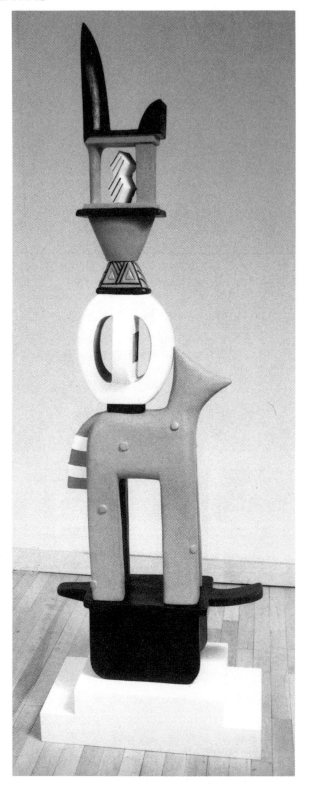

Elyse Saperstein. Elkins Park, Pennsylvania. OPPOSITE: "Tambo," 75 × 24 × 13 inches. ABOVE: "Group of Flowers," 47 × 65 × 6 inches. Photos by John Carlano.

When her work is in the bone-dry state, Elyse Saperstein brushes on terra sigillatas, slips, and, in a few areas, glaze. Cone 03.

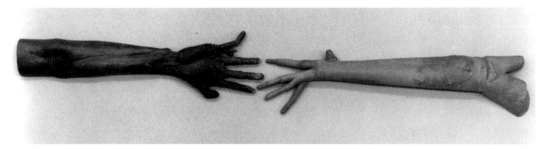

Jacquie Germano. Palmyra, New York. ''Synapse,'' 6 feet long. Photo by Neil Sjobloom.

The soft-looking surface of terra sigillata is used effectively in this piece.

Jacquie Germano. Palmyra, New York. "Metamorphic Spiral III," 40 × 22 × 13 inches. Photo by Walt Chase.

The combination of terra sigillata with copper and cast stone has been used to produce a strong sculptural imagery in this piece. The ceramic elements were fired to cone 06.

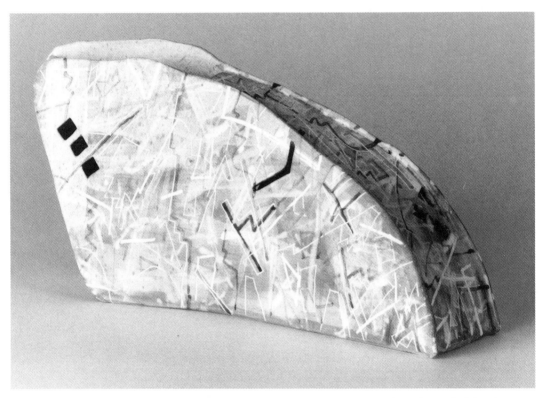

Richard Zakin. Oswego, New York. "Pierced Vase," 14.5 × 27 × 7.2 cm. Photo by T. C. Eckersley.

A highly painted terra sigillata was combined with sgraffito to create this imagery.

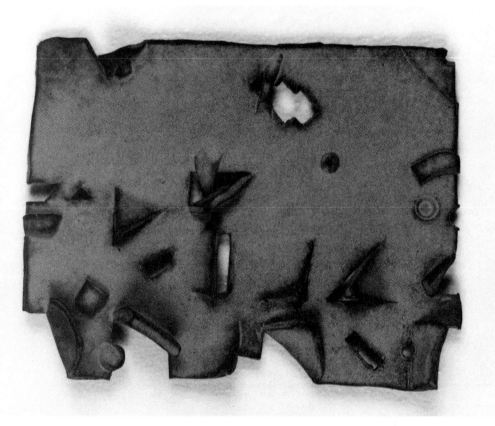

Richard Zakin. Oswego, New York. "Small Tile," 14.2 × 10 cm. Photo by T. C. Eckersley.

A very liquid terra sigillata was applied with a sprayer to achieve the low-viscosity effects. The sigillata flowed away from the edges of the form, leaving a thin dark line in these places.

Anna Calluori Holcombe. Brockport, New York. ABOVE: "Still Life I," 11 × 17 × 2 inches. OPPOSITE: "Tondo II," 18 inches in diameter. Photos by Jim Dusen.

Anna Calluori Holcombe relies on sprayed terra sigillatas to produce a rich surface that never obscures sculptural detail. Cone 04.

Cathie Murdaugh. Charlestown, South Carolina. TOP: ''Pueblo Egg,'' 5 × 4 × 4 inches. RIGHT: ''Cliff Palace Egg,'' 13 × 8 × 8 inches. Photos by Fred McElveen.

Murdaugh paints her forms with terra sigillatas and burnishes them with a river stone, further emphasizing the natural character of the piece.

COLORED SLIPS

Alec Karros. Lafayette, Colorado. "Vase with Flower Arrangement," 16 inches high. Photo by John Woodin.

Karros uses colored slips under a clear glaze to create a rich imagery. Cone 6.

John Stephenson. Ann Arbor, Michigan. ABOVE: ''Helices Entwined #1,'' 14½ × 19½ × 15½ inches. Photo by Dick Schwarze. OPPOSITE: ''Helices Entwined #2,'' 17 × 20 × 15 inches. Photo by Suzanne Coles.

Using thick applications of colored slips, finished with a coating of a clear glaze, Stephenson creates a complex, exciting surface. Cone 03.

Susanne Stephenson. Ann Arbor, Michigan. ABOVE: ''Winter Ocean II,'' 14½ × 22⅕ × 15 inches. OPPOSITE: ''Winterstorm,'' 12½ × 10½ × 9 inches. Photos by Suzanne Coles.

Stephenson establishes her imagery with heavy clay slips. She also uses shinier glazes and vitreous engobes for contrast. Cone 03.

Marylyn Dintenfass. New Rochelle, New York. ABOVE: "Diegma Series: Cobalt," 30 × 32 × 7 inches. OPPOSITE: "Diegma Series: Chrome," 29 × 31 × 8 inches. Photos by Nick Saraco.

In these two pieces Dintenfass has used slips for a great deal of the imagery. She has relied on them to help her create a dry, paint-like imagery. Cone 2.

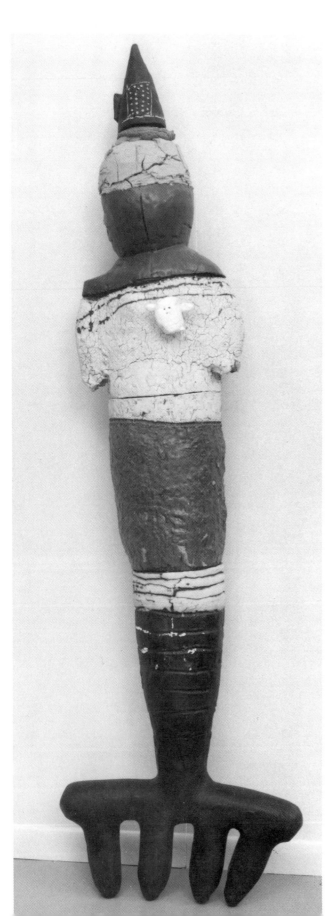

William Stewart. Hamlin, New York.
"Rake," 73 × 26 × 12 inches.

William Stewart applies a preliminary layer of glaze and fires the piece. He then applies slips and more glazes to this fired surface (often using heavy applications). His surfaces are heavily manipulated to encourage rich, abraided results. Cone 04 to 03.

GLAZES

Jo Ann Schnabel. Cedar Falls, Iowa. "Transcendent," 28 × 18 × 16 inches. Photo by William Drescher.

Schnabel relies on her brush-applied glazes, which are at once highly practical and very exciting, to finish her pieces. Irregular, asymmetric forms characterize her work. Cone 3.

Victor Spinski. Newark, Delaware. ''I Am Giving Up Painting,'' 19 × 14 × 10 inches. Photo by Butch Hullet.

Spinski uses glazes, decals, and lusters to replicate common, everyday objects. He fires his glazes to cone 04, while the decals and luster glazes are fired at cone 018.

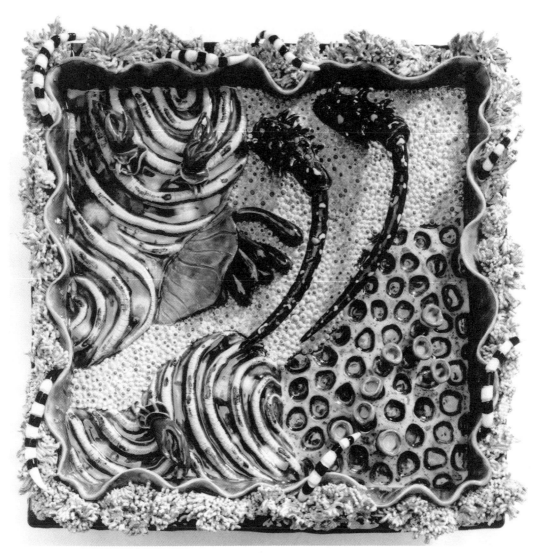

Andrea Johnson. Carmel, California. "Square Tile," 8 × 8 inches. Courtesy Winfield Gallery, Carmel, California. Photo by Lee Hocker.

Andrea Johnson combines studio-made and commercially prepared low fire glazes to achieve rich glaze surfaces. She fires to cone 06 to 05; most pieces are multi-fired.

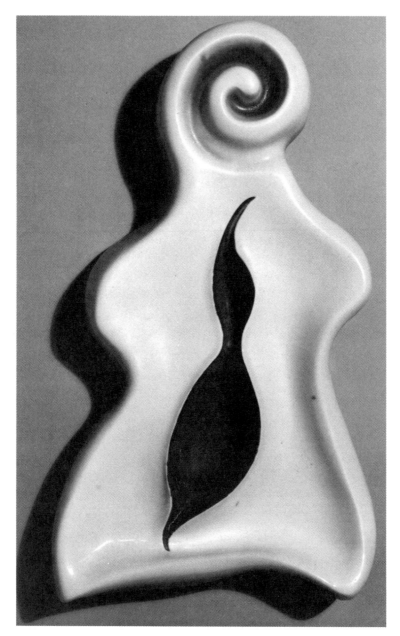

Robin Leventhal. Ann Arbor, Michigan. ''Centrifuge,'' 19 × 11 × 3 inches.

Leventhal's surfaces are derived from sprayed colored slips and clear glazes. These surfaces are smooth, unbroken, and shiny. Their cool, ''industrial'' look fits well with her carefully worked out forms. Cone 6.

Eileen Lewenstein. Brighton, England. "Turning Together," 13 inches high.

Eileen Lewenstein's glazes flow and "break up" richly over the surface of her pieces. She applies her glazes with a sponge and a brush and fires her work to 1250°C (cone 8 to 9).

TWO APPROACHES TO CERAMIC SURFACES: Commercial Preparation and Studio Preparation

The ceramist can make glazes in the studio or buy commercially prepared glazes that are ready to apply to the piece. Either choice influences the look of the surface, and each one has its advantages. This decision has a particularly strong impact on the ceramist working in the electric kiln: most commercially prepared slips and glazes are made with the oxidation atmosphere in mind. In recent years these have become very popular, especially in North America. Therefore the ceramist who works in the electric kiln should know more about the characteristics of both studio-made and commercially prepared surfaces.

COMMERCIALLY PREPARED GLAZES

Commercially prepared glazes are already mixed and ready to use. Studio ceramists who use them benefit from the convenience these materials offer. Many studio ceramists have found these glazes so appealing that they have moved to the low fire just to be able to use them. Photos of pieces made with commercial glazes, finishing underglazes, and lusters appear beginning on pages 81, 102, and 106.

Commercially prepared glazes were originally intended for use by those working in low-fire slipware (often called ''hobby ceramics''), but in the last decade many studio ceramists have adopted them. They offer varied glaze character and visual texture and their colors can be extremely vivid. These glazes can be used to create a wide variety of colors and images—so many in fact that it takes considerable expertise to exploit their possibilities.

Perhaps because they originated outside the fine arts, commercial glazes are somewhat controversial. Many ceramists will not use commercial glazes because of their flamboyant colors and textures; others simply object to the idea of using commercial preparations that have been made under factory conditions. Other ceramists love them, delighting in their wide color range, their reliability, and their interesting image-creating possibilities. These glazes, so different from studio-prepared mixtures, have made us take another look at the way we think about ceramics. They have had a strong influence on the way we think ceramic work should look and how ceramic imagery should be created.

Commercial glazes are finely ground and contain additives (such as gums and colloids) that make them especially appropriate for brush and spray application. As a result, they are easy to apply (they have been termed ''user-friendly''). The viscous consistency of these glazes lends itself well to brush application, while spray applications (including airbrush applications) are aided by the fine grind and excellent suspension of these glazes. They usually are sold in small amounts, and you will want to assemble a group of twenty to fifty glazes from which to choose.

Manufacturers have gone to great efforts to make the color in the jar resemble the color of the glaze after firing. In effect, these glazes are WYSIWYG (what you see [before firing] is what you get [after firing]). Many applications tend to be quite painterly and rely on the WYSIWYG character to relay a true picture of the glaze imagery before it is fired.

STUDIO-MADE GLAZES

Unlike low-fire commercial glazes, most studio-made glazes are not finely ground and do not contain the additives that make brush application so easy. These glazes instead are applied by dipping, pouring, or spraying (using sprayers that can handle the comparatively coarse mix) and rarely are applied with a brush. Photos of pieces with studio-made glazes begin on page 89.

Ceramists who are resistant to using commercial preparations feel that they can control their own ceramic destiny by mixing their own glazes.

When working in this way the ceramist usually makes glazes in fairly large amounts and will assemble a group of eight to fifteen to choose from. Also, studio-made glazes are not WYSIWYG but, rather, reveal their color only when fired. The ceramist rarely will use them with applications that require having a true picture of the imagery before it is fired.

Studio-made glazes encourage simple, strong, and direct imagery. In a natural and vigorous way they reveal their earthy origin, an attribute many ceramists value.

COMBINING COMMERCIAL AND STUDIO-MADE GLAZES

Studio-made and commercially prepared low-fire glazes can easily be applied on the same piece. This strategy is especially useful if the ceramist wishes to combine a brush application (using commercial mixtures) with a spray, dip, or pour application (using studio-made glazes). In this way the ceramist can combine the economy of studio-made glazes with the exciting colors and textures of commercial formulations. See the photos beginning on page 97.

While at times the two camps have been at odds, we seem to have arrived at a point where ceramists employing the two strategies coexist amicably. Both approaches seem valid to me, and contemporary ceramists have created wonderful work using both. Therefore I try to treat these two different approaches to ceramic work with respect and affection.

MAKING STUDIO-MADE GLAZES

Glazes prepared in the studio are economical and give the process a highly individual character. They require a small investment in glaze materials and take time to mix, but the results can be striking.

The ceramist often will assemble a group of eight to fifteen glazes to work with. The applications chosen rarely require a true picture of the imagery before it is fired because these glazes do not reveal their color or character before firing. Application methods include dipping, pouring, and spraying. Studio-made glazes applied using these methods can produce rich imagery that harmonizes with the form rather than dominating it.

To make studio-prepared glazes you will need:

- A selection of materials for making glazes in 5,000- to 20,000-gram lots. The following materials are a minimum requirement: flint, a soda feldspar, spodumene, a soda frit, a boron frit, a light-colored clay (ball clay or kaolin), a stoneware clay, a red clay, dolomite, Gerstley borate, titanium, whiting, and zinc.

- A selection of colorants. Minimum requirements are copper carbonate, cobalt oxide, iron oxide, and rutile. (These are usually purchased in 1,000- to 5,000-gram lots because they are generally required in amounts of 2 to 5 percent.)

- A safety mask approved for use with fine-particle dust.

- An accurate scale, with measuring pan, calibrated in grams and designed for scientific use.

- A container for mixing the glaze materials after they have been weighed. The container must be large enough to hold the entire recipe.

- Water (for suspending the glaze).

- A fine sieve, either 50 or 80 mesh (50 or 80 strands to the inch).

- A coarse sieve (of the type found in a supermarket). This is especially useful if you are making up a large amount of glaze (more than 2,000 grams).

- A clean bristle brush or a rubber spatula (for pushing glaze through the sieve).

- A waterproof marker for labeling the glaze container.

The Process

- Put on your dust mask. Gather the materials for the glaze, and make sure you have enough of each one.

- Make sure that the scale with the measuring pan in place is at the zero point. If it is not, adjust the scale's tare compensation so that it reads zero. Place the material in the measuring pan.

- After weighing, transfer the material to the mixing container and place the next material in the measuring pan. Mix the glaze with enough water to make a creamy mixture.

- Force the glaze through a sieve with a stiff brush or a rubber spatula to homogenize the mixture and get rid of any lumps. If you have made up a large amount of glaze (more than 2,000 grams), speed up the process by passing the mixture through the coarse sieve before using the fine sieve. Add more water if you wish.

- Label the finished glaze. Include its name, color, firing cone, the amount mixed, and the date.

Safety Precautions

When mixing the glaze, wear an effective dust mask; wear gloves or wash your hands thoroughly after mixing. Wear a smock while you work or change your clothing afterward.

After glazing, sponge down tabletops and mop the studio floor. If your studio is equipped with a ventilation fan—and it *should* be—turn it on and keep it on during the mixing and cleaning procedures.

RICH SURFACES FROM STUDIO-MADE GLAZES

Most glazes fired in oxidation have little modulation or visual texture, and often the ceramist will want a visually textured surface. Fortunately, a number of effective methods can be used to produce visually textured glazes in oxidation.

Recipe Types Useful for Creating Rich Surfaces

A number of glaze types especially useful for creating complex glaze imagery present interesting challenges to the ceramist:

- *Ash glazes:* these glazes are characterized by light-colored spots, blooms of color, and patterns of running glaze.

- *Calcium/magnesium flowing glazes:* these cone 9 glazes are marked by rich textures and strong glaze flow.

- *Low-fire mat glazes:* these mat surfaces are derived from materials that encourage a mat surface but do not compromise stability.

- *Flowing mat glazes:* these glazes rely on materials that do not derive their mat qualities from alumina; they are marked by strong glaze flow patterns.

- *Crystal glazes:* these glazes contain zinc or titanium and are fired in such a way as to encourage the growth of crystals during cooling.

- *Dry-textured crawling glazes:* these high-magnesium mixtures (50–60%) crawl and curl to produce a rich surface.

- *Texturizing overglaze sprays:* these glazes are applied over other glazes to encourage visual texture.

Wood Ash Glazes

Ash is created by burning wood, bark, straw, hay, reeds, or other organic materials in an open fire. (Avoid the less interesting wood ash from an airtight stove.) Wood ash is added to glazes to encourage strong visual textures. It derives its visual textures from the granular character of the ash and from its calcium and phosphorus content. Ash varies greatly depending on its source, the season, and the environment from which it was gathered. While the ingredients rarely vary (silica, alumina, calcium, phosphorus, and trace elements), the proportions can vary a great deal. One batch of wood ash will never act exactly like another, nor can you count on this year's batch to act like last year's batch. Therefore always test the wood ash before applying it to a piece.

A Wood Ash Test

Gather enough wood ash to make the experiment worthwhile. Dry-mix the wood ash, but first follow the safety precautions in the section below on working with wood ash and wood ash glazes.

Add samples of wood ash in 10- and 40-gram amounts to 100 grams of the following glazes:

- a high-silica recipe

- a high-alumina recipe

- a high-melter recipe

- a dark-clay recipe

In some cases the resulting mixture will be quite dry and unmelted, in others overmelted, but still others will produce the rich texture and flowing patterns of a successful ash glaze.

This test is an effective way to determine which glaze types will work with a particular batch of wood ash.

Applying Wood Ash Glazes

Wood ash glazes can be applied by dipping, pouring, brushing, or spraying. Most spray guns quickly become clogged when used to spray the coarse particles of wood ash glazes. Instead, try the Paasche model L sprayer, which has an almost unblockable external-mix configuration.

Safety When Working with Wood Ash and Glazes Containing Wood Ash

While the wood ash is in the dry state, wear a dust mask with filters designed to trap fine-particle dust. Wear disposable protective outerware (look for inexpensive raincoat-like garments at industrial supply houses). While the wood ash is in the wet state, wear rubber gloves.

Always wear a mask when spraying wood ash glazes. To combat dust, wipe work surfaces with a wet sponge and clean the floor with a wet mop. Do this frequently as you work.

Cone 9 Calcium/Magnesium Flowing Glazes

Calcium/magnesium glaze materials have a dual nature in that they are quite refractory (nonmelting) until cone 8; then, at cone 8 and above, they become strong melters. They encourage strong visual textures, which are characterized by a rich pattern of rivulets that play over the surface of the glaze. It is my feeling that a cone 9 firing temperature is more significant in shaping the look of a glaze than is kiln atmosphere and that calcium/magnesium glazes will have a similar look regardless of whether they are fired in oxidation or reduction.

Appropriate amounts of calcium/magnesium-containing materials for cone 9 glazes: dolomite, magnesium carbonate, whiting—15–30%; calcium/magnesium silicates (wollastonite, talc)—25–50%.

Low-Fire Mat Recipes

In the past, low-fire mat glazes formulated with lead or barium were fairly common. Lead lends itself to good low-fire mats because it smooths high-clay mat glazes while simultaneously providing good fluxing power to create a rich mat surface. Barium encourages the formation of microcrystals, which break up the glaze surface and impart its mat effect. Today we want to avoid recipes that contain such toxic materials. Unfortunately low-fire mat recipes are difficult to formulate without these dangerous materials.

In recent years some ceramists have experimented with strontium mat glazes. The toxicity of strontium is debatable, but it appears to present only a small danger to the ceramist. Strontium is somewhat expensive and recipes that call for its use are hard to find (I include a few in the recipe section).

I have also experimented with zirconium opacifiers, now in common use, which work well in glazes and are not toxic. If used in amounts ranging from 15 to 25 percent, zirconium opacifiers effectively encourage mat glazes. I have developed a number of successful recipes using this strategy, and I include a few in the recipe section.

Flowing Mat Recipes

Flowing mat glazes are unusual. Mat glazes generally derive their mat character from high clay amounts, and recipes high in clay are not free-flowing. Flowing mat glazes, however, derive their matness from an abundance of weak melters in the recipe. Their low alumina amounts encourage strong glaze flow. These recipes are likely to be unstable and difficult to use. They will often flow off the work and onto the kiln shelf, welding the work to the shelf. For this reason I do not recommend them for classroom use. On the other hand, their low alumina content encourages rich, varied color and surface.

These extremely beautiful glazes are certainly worthy of exploration.I discovered recipes of this type in the book *Grande Feu Céramique* by Taxile Doat, a French ceramist active in the early 1900s.* In this excellent book Doat discusses flowing mat glazes and lists a number of recipes (one of which is included below, adapted for modern use).

Mat Ivory Yellow (a flowing mat glaze, cone 9 oxidation)

soda feldspar	30	whiting	14
kaolin	11	rutile	8
ground silica (flint)	37		

*Taxile Doat. *Grande Feu Céramique,* trans. Samuel Robineau (Syracuse, N.Y.: Keramic Studio Publishing, 1905).

If you experiment with this strongly flowing glaze, place a tile made from soft brick or a piece of broken kiln shelf under the work. Paint the surface of the tile with a coating of kiln wash (a mixture of kaolin and flint).

Crystal Glazes

Crystal glazes are marked by the presence of metallic crystals that form on the surface of the fired glaze. They are created by adding titanium or zinc to a low-alumina glaze recipe. Appropriate amounts are 6–10 percent titanium and 2–8 percent zinc.

Crystal growth requires a long soaking period and careful temperature control during the latter part of the fire. It is important to use a pyrometer to observe any changes in kiln temperature (see page 231).

Because the low-alumina recipes flow quite freely, the kiln shelves must be protected from excess glaze flow during the firing. Place a tile made from soft brick or a piece of broken kiln shelf under the work and paint the surface of the tile with a coating of kiln wash (a mixture of kaolin and flint).

A Crystal Glaze Firing

1 Place each piece on a slab of soft brick or on a piece of broken kiln shelf.

2 Fire the kiln in the normal fashion and allow the temperature to reach the desired range.

3 Turn off the kiln and allow it to cool for 20 minutes.

4 Monitor the temperature inside the kiln using the pyrometer. Hold the temperature steady for two to four hours. It is during this period that the zinc or titanium crystals will have a chance to develop.

In his book Taxile Doat also discusses crystal glazes and provides recipes (the one below has been adapted for modern use).

Mat Crystalline Yellow Brown (a crystal glaze, cone 9 oxidation)

soda feldspar	26	whiting	12
kaolin	10	rutile	7
ground silica (flint)	37	red iron oxide	7

Dry-Textured Crawling Glazes

Recently some ceramists have become fascinated with glazes that produce heavy crawling textures. The striking and unusual surfaces are only partially vitrified and are dry-textured, deeply fissured, parched, and curdled. Often parts of the clay body are revealed where the glaze has pulled or flaked away. These essentially underfired low- and mid-fire glazes contain a high percentage of magnesium carbonate (as much as 60 percent). In the early part of the firing the magnesium loses water and shrinks to create strong textural effects. The result is very striking imagery. Below is a typical recipe:

Islip 2   Cone 3   Richard Zakin

soda frit	24	magnesium carbonate	46
ball	8	spodumene	12
Gerstley borate	8	titanium	2

Overglaze Sprays That Encourage Visual Textures

Unlike the recipes described above, recipes for overglazes are not meant to be used as base glazes; rather, they are applied over other glazes, usually by spraying. When applied, they react with the base glaze to promote a rich and complex visual texture. The texture is an ''orange peel'' pattern of light and dark modulation.

The essential ingredients in overglaze sprays are lithium (from spodumene), phosphorus (from bone ash), calcium (from bone ash and dolomite), and iron oxide (from the highly impure dark clay). All these surfaces definitely have an ''oxidation look,'' but they can be very pleasing in appearance.

Overglaze recipes are best applied by spraying because the spray encourages the formation of the orange-peel texture. (Use a nonclogging external-mix sprayer.)

Materials That Encourage Rich Surfaces

Many ceramists who work in the oxidation fire, especially in the mid- and high-fire range, rely on materials added to the recipe that encourage visual texture. These materials are: (1) spodumene (a lithium feldspar), which is characterized by light-colored spots and patterns of running glaze; (2) titanium, which, like spodumene, is characterized by light-colored spots and patterns of running glaze; and (3) granular rutile and illmenite, which are characterized by dark, peppery spots.

Granular Rutile or Ilmenite.   Granular rutile and the similar granular ilmenite are both iron/titanium compounds (ilmenite, however, contains a greater percentage of iron). In their granular form both can be added to glazes (1–3% additions are recommended) to create a tight pattern of small black spots. (Daniel Rhodes, in his book *Clay and Glazes for the Potter*, called them ''peppery'' in appearance.) The effect can be subtle and pleasingly irregular.

Lithium-Containing Materials (spodumene and lithium carbonate).   Lithium-containing materials encourage strong visual textures. We derive lithium from spodumene (a feldspar that contains lithium) and from lithium carbonate. Of the two materials, spodumene is preferable because the lithium in spodumene is locked into the compound in a way that minimizes inhalation and ingestion problems.

Lithium is a strong melter at every part of the firing spectrum, and it is useful in the low fire. Lithium carbonate and, to a lesser extent, spodumene are low in viscosity and discourage pinholing.

Titanium.   Small amounts of titanium (.5–2 percent) encourage a strong pattern of visual texture and cause strong melts. Sources of titanium are titanium dioxide, rutile, and some highly impure clays.

Spodumene/Titanium Combinations.   Both spodumene and titanium encourage strong visual textures and work well together. They are especially admirable partners because spodumene discourages pinholing, thus offsetting titanium's tendency to encourage pinholing. Suggested percentages: spodumene, 12–24 percent, titanium, 6–12 percent.

GLAZE PROBLEMS

While the oxidation fire generally produces stable, durable results, it is simply in the nature of ceramics that you will encounter various problems at one time or another as you pursue your work. Among them are crawling, sedimenting, crazing, shivering, and running.

Crawling

Glaze crawling is marked by patches of bare clay alternating with areas of glaze. The areas of glaze, furthermore, are often marked by cracks and fissures. In most cases crawling is a glaze flaw, although some ceramists use crawled glazes as an integral and highly valued part of their imagery.

Crawling can occur when the glaze has been overflocculated; that is, the glaze is too sticky and shrinks too much. In such a case, the potter may substitute calcined clay for some of the clay in the recipe (see Calcining, page 30). Crawling can also occur when the glaze layer is too thick or when the pot is too wet or too dusty, or when a wet glaze is applied over a very dry glaze. If the glaze is too thick, thin it with water. If the piece is too wet (perhaps you have rinsed off a glaze application), let it dry for a few hours before trying to glaze it again. If the piece is too dusty, dust the surface with a damp sponge. If you intend to apply multiple layers of glaze, let the first glaze set, but do not let it dry completely.

Sedimenting

Some glazes, especially those containing frits, bone ash, and lithium, sink to the bottom of the bucket and harden there. This phenomenon, called sedimentation, can make it difficult to use some glazes on a continuing basis. Sedimented glazes can cause real problems in a classroom situation because most students will not take the time to break up the sedimented layers. If the student tries to use the glaze anyway, the fired result can be quite surprising, for some of the most important glaze materials will remain in the sedimented layers.

Two opposing solutions have been proposed for this problem: flocculation and deflocculation. Flocculation is suggested to help keep the glaze's clay content in suspension. Deflocculation is suggested to break up the sedimentation process. In my experience, deflocculation is more effective. You may add 2 percent epsom salts (magnesium sulfate) or magnesium carbonate to deflocculate a glaze.

Crazing

Crazing occurs when the glaze shrinks more than the clay body. When this happens, the brittle glaze reacts to the stress by cracking. These numerous fine cracks create a web of fine lines that form a geometric pattern. Though crazing weakens a glaze and can render it less durable on utilitarian ware, the crazing pattern can be pleasing to the eye. Some ceramists try intentionally to create crazing rather than trying to avoid it. To avoid crazing, use glazes that are high in silica-containing materials, such as ground silica (flint), feldspars, and frits. Also, avoid materials that contain high amounts of sodium, such as soda frits and soda feldspars.

To encourage crazing, use a glaze that is high in flux and contains sodium, a high-shrinkage material. Select glazes that contain 40 to 55 percent of fluxes such as Gerstley borate, whiting, and magnesium carbonate and 40 to 50 percent of high-soda feldspar or frit.

Shivering

Shivering, the exact opposite of crazing, occurs when the clay body shrinks more than the glaze. The glaze, in a state of compression, buckles and small pieces flake away from the surface of the piece. Shivering is usually evidenced first at the sharp edges of the form (such as at the lip, throwing lines, and handles). You may not notice any shivering when you take the piece from the kiln; it may take a month or two for the pressure to build and cause the glaze to buckle and peel. Magnification, however, may reveal buckling before it is visible to the naked eye. A common culprit here is an excess of lithium in the glaze (lithium does not shrink and can even encourage glaze expansion). More than 3 percent lithium carbonate or 35 percent spodumene can cause shivering. Shivering also occurs when the ceramist has used an "open" clay body that shrinks very little. If shivering occurs, test your clay body for absorption. If it is more than 8 percent, the body is "open": in this case, changing the body recipe will help.

Running

Running is the uncontrolled flow of the glaze during firing. Glazes may flow so much that the piece becomes welded to the kiln shelf. Most ceramists discard highly flowing glazes (if necessary, they can be used, but protect the shelves by placing the ware on firing stilts). To test for excessive running, place an ample amount of glaze at the top of a vertically placed tile; if it flows heavily to the bottom of the tile, it is highly flowing.

Problems Associated with Multifiring Reglazing

Either to take advantage of multifire techniques or to rescue a piece whose glaze is not successful, you will want to be able to apply another layer of glaze to an already glazed piece. Reglazing can be difficult because our glazes are generally formulated to be applied to the absorbent surface of unfired or bisque-fired clay. It is difficult to make glazes of normal, rather liquid consistency adhere to the completely nonabsorbent surface of an already-glazed piece. Fortunately a number of strategies have been worked out to address this problem.

The most common strategy is to apply a normal glaze to a heated piece; applied with care, enough glaze will adhere to build up a useful layer. The glaze is best applied with a sprayer, although pour and splash methods may also work.

Another, more useful approach is to alter the viscosity of the wet glaze. Glazes for china painting and commercially prepared luster glazes, which are suspended in a thickened turpentine, can be applied easily over a fired surface. These glazes will require application techniques different from those for glazes of normal consistency, but they will lend themselves well to the reglazing process. Wear a face mask when applying these glaze preparations. Water-based china paints are in the process of being developed, but at present they are more difficult to apply.

COMMERCIAL LOW-FIRE GLAZES

The studio ceramist who wishes to work with commercially prepared glazes has a great many choices regarding suppliers and glaze types. These preparations are widely available, but they are especially common in North America, where they are made by a number of large firms. The manufacturers try to cover a wide field and produce many types of engobe, glaze, and underglaze preparations. Each type is usually made in twenty to forty different colors and textures.

Commercially prepared glazes should be applied in three or more coats, either with a brush or sprayer. When brushed, they should be applied using opposing brushstrokes for each coat (the first coat horizontal, the second vertical, and the last, again, horizontal).

Following are descriptions of the types of commercial glazes available.

Glossy Glazes

Glossy glazes represent the standard glaze line of low-fire commercial glazes. They feature bright color and are at their best when applied to white clay bodies (especially low-fire, high-talc bodies). Their makers recommend a heavy coating of three applications, often using opposing brushstrokes. For the best gloss, they should be fired quickly.

Mat Glazes

Mat glazes have a satin mat surface and are often more limited in color and less bright than the shiny glazes. Their firing range is often somewhat higher than other low-fire glazes, and they may be at their most effective when fired to cone 02. A slow firing and long cooling are usually recommended.

Opalescent Glazes

Opalescent glazes have a high gloss and a strong metallic and opalescent character. A fast firing is recommended to encourage the opalescent effect. These glazes should be applied in multiple coatings over a dark clay body. Because they flow a good deal, their color can vary, thus emphasizing any marks in the clay form.

Variegated Glazes

Variegated glazes contain materials that encourage visual texture. In some cases these materials are fine grained and easily remain in suspension during brush application. In other cases the glaze base contains large crystal additions of a contrasting color; the crystals sink to the bottom of the container and must be stirred up from the bottom with a brush (these glazes are not meant for spray application). The crystals are also sold separately to add to any prepared glaze. Many variegated glazes flow a good deal, which means they will smooth over application inconsistencies. A variation on this type contrasts shiny glaze crystals with a mat-surface glaze to produce a highly varied glaze surface.

Crackle Glazes

Crackle glazes shrink during the cooling cycle (which should be rapid for best results), resulting in crackling (sometimes called crazing). While not appropriate for any objects that might conceivably be used for holding food, these glazes are appropriate for nonutilitarian pieces and sculpture.

Dimensional Glazes

Dimensional glazes produce a raised image. They are meant to be used to create linear effects and to this end are packaged in plastic squeeze bottles. They are most effective when applied over the glazes.

Pebble Glazes

Pebble glazes form a regular texture of "droplets" on a smooth ground. The droplets tend to be more glassy than the ground. These glazes should be applied with a brush or sprayer in three coats. The surface is not appropriate for pieces that will be used to hold food.

Underglazes

Underglaze colors are made from colorants or stains and a binder. They come in a wide range of color, and the colors can be mixed and blended. These stains lend themselves to a variety of effects and can be quite painterly. They may be applied to either greenware or bisque-fired ware. For permanence, they must be covered with a glaze, usually a clear glaze. They are best used with a clear glaze supplied by the manufacturer.

The ceramist may choose from transparent, translucent, and opaque underglazes. Translucent underglazes reveal the character of the brushstroke; therefore it is important to apply them directly in one stroke. They are formulated so that only one application is necessary. The resulting effect is similar to that of watercolor painting.

Underglaze Chalks and Pencils for Decorating

In composition, underglaze chalks and pencils are similar to other underglazes, but their form encourages the linear and shaded imagery that we associate with pencils and chalks used on paper. They are perhaps at their best when used with painted or sprayed underglazes. As in other underglazes, the binder will not protect them from smearing after firing and they must be covered with a clear glaze.

Finishing Underglazes (Velvets)

Finishing underglazes can be used like regular underglazes and covered with a clear glaze before firing. Unlike normal underglazes, however, they contain fluxes that harden them. Therefore, when used as the finishing surface of the piece, they do not need to be finished with a clear top glaze. In this case their surface will be a rich and painterly soft mat. While fairly durable, these surfaces are not safe for food, and they are *not* suitable for application on utilitarian pieces. Photos of pieces made with finishing underglazes begin on page 102.

Overglazes

Also known as china paints or enamels, overglazes are meant to be applied to pieces already fired to maturity, usually over a fired glaze. They can be applied with a brush, a fine-textured sponge, or sprayer and are at their best when used for linear and painterly imagery. A smooth, unbroken application over a large area is more difficult to achieve, but it can be accomplished using a fine-textured sponge or a sprayer. Most overglaze paints are suspended in an oily base (often in "fat oil," a thickened turpentine). The oily base has a strong odor that requires good ventilation, and some may find it offensive. Water-based china paints do not have these unpleasant side effects, but, unfortunately, they are not so easily applied. China paints are fired to a very low temperature (cones 018 to 016).

Metallic Overglazes and Lusters

Lusters are metallic overglazes and are either opaque or transparent. The opaque lusters are thin metallic coatings that look almost like applications of a silver, gold, or copper metallic foil. The transparent lusters modify the color and surface character of the underlying glaze. As a result, when light is reflected off a translucent lustered glaze surface, the surface will retain the color of the base glaze but will be highly reflective, metallic, and iridescent. Photos of pieces made with lusters begin on page 106.

Susanne Stephenson. Ann Arbor, Michigan. "Storm Beach I," 14 × 19 × 15 inches. Photo by Suzanne Coles.

Susanne Stephenson applies her imagery with a brush and a painting knife. The vigor of this application is unusual in the ceramic medium. Cone 03.

OPPOSITE ABOVE:
Virginia Cartwright.
Pasadena, California.
"Group of Clay Inlay
Pieces."

*Cartwright has been an
advocate of colored clay
inlay techniques for a number of years. In her work
she exploits the strength of
this method, creating surface, form, and color at the
same time. Cone 3–5.*

OPPOSITE BELOW:
Angelo di Petta. Toronto,
Ontario, Canada. Platter,
9 × 9 inches. Photo by
Chris Chown.

*Di Petta creates his com-
plex imagery using slips,
stains, and glazes and a
wide range of application
strategies. A series of photographs showing his
methods appears in
Chapter 7.*

RIGHT:
JoAnn Schnabel. Cedar
Falls, Iowa. "Impulse," 43
× 19 × 18 inches.

*In this piece Schnabel con-
trasts unglazed segments
with brush-applied, glazed
areas. Cone 3.*

Alec Karros. Lafayette,
Colorado. "Soup Services,"
10 inches (diameter).

*Karros's work is brilliantly
colored and glazed. The
result is a personal reinter-
pretation of traditional
thrown forms. Cone 6.*

George Mason. Newcastle,
Maine. Wall piece, Greely
High School, North
Yarmouth, Maine, 4 × 4
feet. Photo by Dennis
Griggs.

*In this piece Mason has
contrasted unglazed terra-
cotta elements with a
smooth-surfaced glaze.
Cone 02.*

James Lovera. Plymouth, California. "Earth Crater Blue Bowl/Over Black Clay," 4 × 9 inches. Courtesy of Winfield Gallery, Carmel, California. Photo by Walter Kennedy.

Lovera combines traditional vessel forms with a black clay body and very active and highly textured glaze surfaces. The forms are fired to cone 6 and the glazes to cone 03.

John Chalke. Calgary, Alberta, Canada. Bowl.

Chalke has pioneered the exploration of the complex reactions that can take place in the fire. The resulting surfaces, as here, can be highly evocative. Cone 6.

Eric James Mellon. Bognor Regis, England. "Portrait Bowl," 14½ inches (diameter). Photo by Chris Hadow Photography.

Mellon has his own complex and compelling visual language. He fires his work to 1300°C (cone 10).

Mathais Osterman. Montreal, Quebec, Canada. "Square Bowl, Boy and Dog," 7½ inches (diameter). Photo by Jan Thijs.

The surface of Osterman's maiolica pieces is somber and expressive, characteristics we do not expect from maiolica. Cone 06.

Ina Orevskaya. St. Petersburg, Russia. Platter. Photo by Richard Zakin.

Orevskaya creates her painted work in porcelain in the tradition of European court porcelain. Her work shows that this demanding technique can be used to create imagery with a strong contemporary feeling. She first fires her work to 1400°C (cone 14) and then fires the imagery and final glaze to 800–850°C (cone 014–012).

David Macdonald. Syracuse, New York. Earthenware plate, Ndebele Series, 16½ inches (diameter).

For some time Macdonald has been using imagery whose sources come from Africa. He begins with terra sigillatas and glazes and finishes his pieces with commercially prepared overglazes. Cone 04.

Greg Pitts. Columbia, South Carolina. Vase, 7 inches high. Photo by Greg Pitts.

In this piece Pitts has painted with water-based overglaze enamels on porcelain to obtain a highly painterly and brilliantly colored image. He fires his work to cone 9/10 and again to cone 019.

Mary Barringer. Shelburne Falls, Massachusetts. Untitled, 7½ × 10½ × 11 inches. Photo by Wayne Fleming.

Working in a light-colored stoneware, Barringer applies dark stains and slips and then uses a sponge to wipe them away. Only that left in the interstices remains. Cone 6.

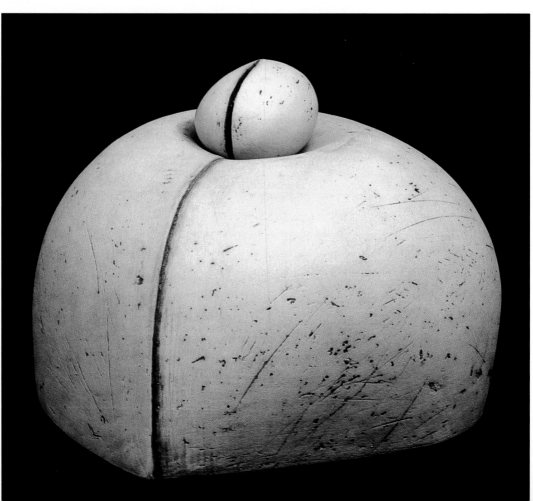

TOXICITY IN COMMERCIAL GLAZES

To achieve desirable color and surface characteristics, especially in the low fire, some low-fire glazes are made with toxic materials such as lead and cadmium. Pieces glazed with these preparations should never be used as containers for food as the glazes may leach the toxic materials. Manufacturers have been concerned about these problems for many years and wherever possible have duplicated the preparations that contain toxic materials with nontoxic versions, thus giving the ceramist a measure of choice. The preparations that contain toxic materials are clearly labeled on the container. Some manufacturers make a special line of nontoxic glazes.

GLAZE FIRING: GENERAL RECOMMENDATIONS

Many low-fire commercially prepared glazes are at their best when fired to cone 06 or 05, but others work well at temperatures up to cone 03. Some preparations require a quick firing and cooling, while others do well in a more normal firing. Directions for the appropriate firing temperature and type of firing are noted in the manufacturer's catalog.

The catalogs available from a number of the large manufacturers are wonderful sources of information. They are colorful, complete, and clearly written. These catalogs are especially helpful because there are so many low-fire glaze types to choose from, each requiring a different firing.

MY EXPERIENCE WITH COMMERCIAL GLAZES

For many years I hesitated using commercial glazes. I love the process of making up and testing new glaze recipes, so why should I let someone else take away my fun? However, in talking with friends and colleagues who have used commercially prepared glazes, I began to realize that they had advantages that could help me in my work. Furthermore, I felt that if I intended to write about these glazes, I should experiment with them firsthand.

Choosing the product I would use was difficult because the various manufacturers make a bewildering variety. Some publish useful pamphlets that I found helpful. I also found my conversations with friends pointed me in the right direction. Martha Holt, a ceramist and friend from western Pennsylvania, was especially helpful. I settled upon Amaco Velvets, which are finishing underglazes that do not require a covering glaze. Many contemporary ceramists use them because they look so much like acrylic paint and come in a wide range of rich colors. Their appearance unfired and fired is almost identical. These glazes are the most WYSIWYG materials I have used in my career as a ceramist. In addition, they are easily and naturally applied and lend themselves to a variety of application techniques and strategies. I apply them with a brush and use them like watercolors, a medium I had a great fondness for before I became a ceramist.

I did run into some problems using these glazes. Sometimes they reminded me so much of paint that I had difficulty using them with relief imagery. My imagery became so painterly that I was in danger of losing touch with the clay character of my work. After some further experimentation, however, I was able to produce a few pieces with imagery I liked. My exploration is still rudimentary, but I continue to use these glazes and look forward to the results.

COMMERCIAL MID-FIRE GLAZES

Recently a number of manufacturers who make low-fire glazes have offered a line of mid-fire glazes as well. These mid-fire preparations have been formulated to make the most of the electric kiln. Though they are a fairly recent development, they seem to be gaining favor. The potential market for these products is significant, and there is no reason they should not find favor with many ceramists, just as their low-fire siblings have.

While the color is not as vivid as that produced in lower-temperature firings, the range of color is still wide. These surfaces can be quite appealing as well as highly durable and stable. It would seem that these practical virtues should be desirable to ceramists who want to use prepared glazes.

Commercially prepared glazes will be particularly useful to the beginner who wishes to work at the mid-fire temperature in an electric kiln and who must work without the support of a teacher because of their virtues of reliability and simplicity.

COMMERCIAL GLAZES

Karen Thuesen Massaro. Santa Cruz, California. ''Bowl #23,'' 5 × 12¾ inches. Photo by Lee Hocker.

In this piece Massaro has made extensive use of glaze pencil along with colorant washes and wax resist. Cone 10.

Sally Gaynor. Santa Cruz, California. OPPOSITE: "Tectonic T" (teapot), 11 × 6½ × 1½ inches. ABOVE: "Between a Rock and a Hard Place" (teapot), 9 × 11 × 6 inches. Courtesy Winfield Gallery, Carmel, California.

Sally Gaynor exploits the reliability and control of commercial glazes and multiple firings to produce her complex painted imagery. Cone 06.

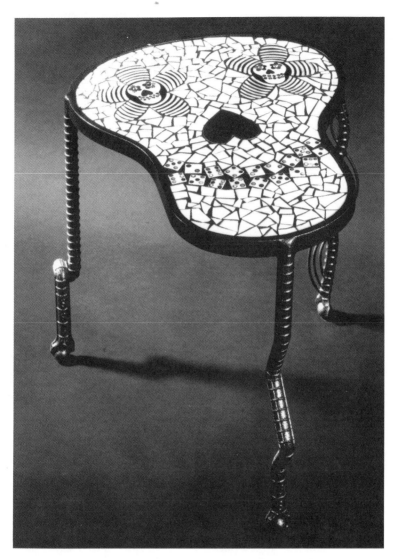

Susie Ketchum. Carmel, California. OPPOSITE: ''Coffee Cup Shrine,'' 36 × 24 inches. Photo by J.C. Wener; cabinetwork by David Overholt. ABOVE: ''Skull Table,'' 18 × 19 × 12 inches. Courtesy Winfield Gallery, Carmel, California. Steelwork by Nils Niemi; photo by Rick Szczecaowski.

Ketchum uses brush-applied, low-fire, commercially produced glazes to create her painted imagery. She fires first to cone 04 and glaze-fires to cone 06.

Sylvia Netzer. New York. ''A Machine for Living I,'' 8½ × 13 × 12 inches. Photo © 1992 by David Lubarsky; all rights reserved.

Netzer uses commercial underglazes to create a bright colored, painterly surface. She has fired this piece to cone 6, which is nominally higher than the maximum for these preparations, but they work quite well at this temperature.

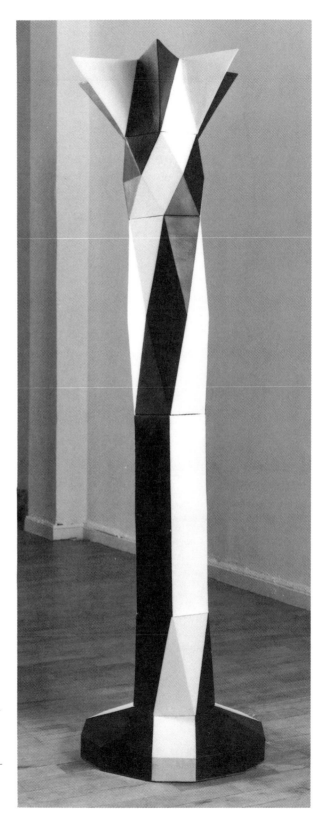

Sylvia Netzer. New York. "Twisting Danger Column," 74½ × 22 × 22 inches. Photo © 1992 by David Lubarsky; all rights reserved.

In this piece Netzer has fired underglazes to cone 5 and then fired another application of underglazes to cone 06.

Virginia Scotchie. Columbia, South Carolina. TOP: "Circle," 23 × 32 × 32 inches. BELOW: "Linear Formations," 18 × 12 × 13 inches. Photos by Todd Livingston.

*Scotchie uses overglaze enamels to finish the surfaces of her sculptural pieces. She fires these to cone
019.*

STUDIO-MADE GLAZES

Richard Zakin. Oswego, New York. ''Footed Vase,'' 12 × 13.5 × 10.5 cm.
Photo by T. C. Eckersley.

*A smooth, enamel-like, studio-made glaze was used to finish this piece.
Cone 6.*

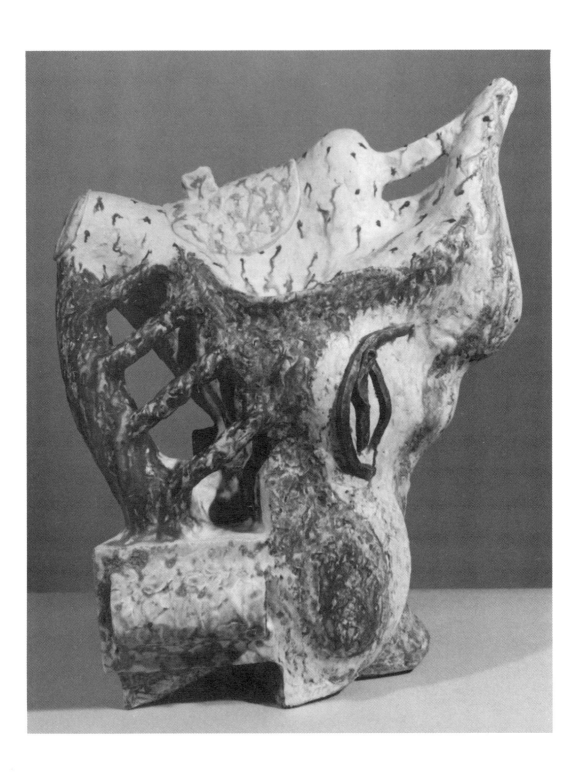

Angus Suttie. London. OPPOSITE: ''Vessel,'' 58 cm. high. ABOVE: ''Significant Accessory,'' 57 cm. high. Photos by the artist.

Suttie uses strongly flowing low-fire glazes to obtain rich, soft-looking surfaces. Much of his work is multi-fired to cone 3.

Lana Wilson. Del Mar, California. "90s Artifact Teapot," 8 × 9 × 3½ inches. Photo by Martin Trailer.

This piece is noteworthy for its dry, rich, and "crumbly" glaze texture. The glazes are applied with a brush and fired at cone 06 or cone 05. Color is generally derived from a cobalt oxide stain.

James Lovera. Plymouth, California. ABOVE: "Pale Blue Lava Bowl," 4½ × 9 inches. BELOW: "Ceramic Bowl, Black and White Bark," 5 × 8½ inches. Photos by Walter Kennedy.

Lovera manipulates his glaze recipes by using materials that are refractory or that encourage local reduction (such as silicon carbide). He alternates layers of melted and refractory surfaces, which strongly interact during the fire. In this way Lovera is able to achieve rich and complex surfaces. He fires his porcelain clay body to a point just short of vitreous (cone 6) and then applies glazes, which are fired to cone 03.

Greg Pitts. Columbia, South Carolina. OPPOSITE: "Vase with Frog Lid," 6 × 7 × 7 inches. ABOVE: "Teapot," 6 × 7 × 5 inches. Photos by Greg Pitts.

In these pieces Pitts used a kind of stain he calls "gōsū" (cobalt stain with iron impurities) painted under a clear glaze. Cone 9/10.

Vladimir Gorislavtsev. St. Petersburg, Russia. "Siberian Scene: Platters," each approximately 35 cm. Photos by Richard Zakin.

Gorislavtsev uses commercial underglaze stains under a clear glaze to create his imagery. He fires first to 1200°C (cone 6) for bisque, then 1000°C (cone 06) for the glaze fire.

COMBINING COMMERCIAL AND STUDIO-MADE GLAZES

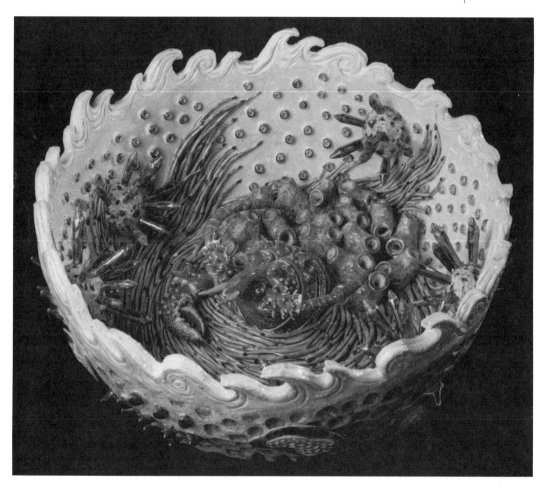

Andrea Johnson. Carmel, California. ''Bowl,'' 1 foot (diameter) × 6½ inches (depth). Courtesy Winfield Gallery, Carmel, California. Photo by Lee Hocker.

Johnson uses low-fire glazes to achieve a sense of the abundance of detail in the natural world. She fires to cone 06/05; most of her work is multi-fired.

Richard Burkett. San Diego, California. "Domestic Logjam," 13 × 18 × 18 inches. Photo by the artist.

In this piece Burkett combines commercially produced glazes and underglazes with studio-made terra sigillatas and glazes. These are applied to a porcelain body fired to cone 6.

Judith Salomon. Cleveland, Ohio. ''Sake Set,'' 15 × 16 × 9 inches. Photo © Nesnadny & Schwartz; all rights reserved.

Salomon combines studio-made and commercial glazes in her highly painted work. She bisque-fires her work to cone 03 and then fires to cone 04 for the glaze fire.

Marisa Recchia. Murfreesboro, Tennessee. LEFT: ''Tripod with Collar and Vessel,'' 48 × 24 inches. BELOW: ''Tripod Plate,'' 12 × 17 inches.

Recchia uses commercially produced glaze stains in a studio-made base glaze to finish her work. Cone 06.

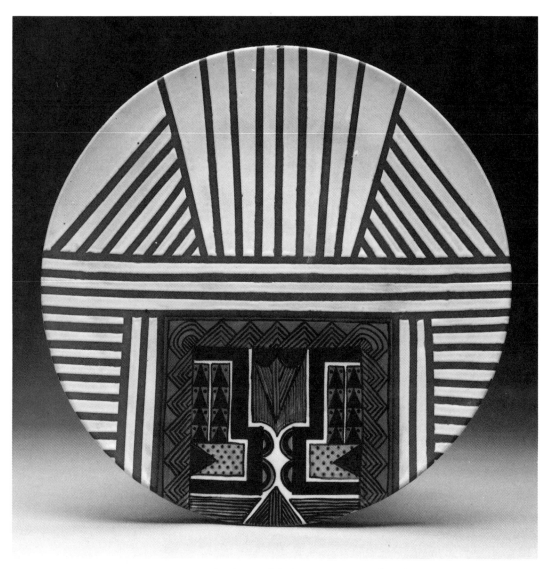

David R. Macdonald. Syracuse, New York. Plate, Ndebele Series, 16½ inches diameter.

Macdonald uses terra sigillatas and commercial underglazes under a clear glaze. Cone 04.

FINISHING UNDERGLAZES

Roy Strassberg. Mankato, Minnesota. "Stonehenge Jazz House #1," 36 × 25 × 4 inches.

Strassberg uses finishing underglazes to create imagery with a strong painterly character. Cone 04 for bisque, cone 06 for the final fire.

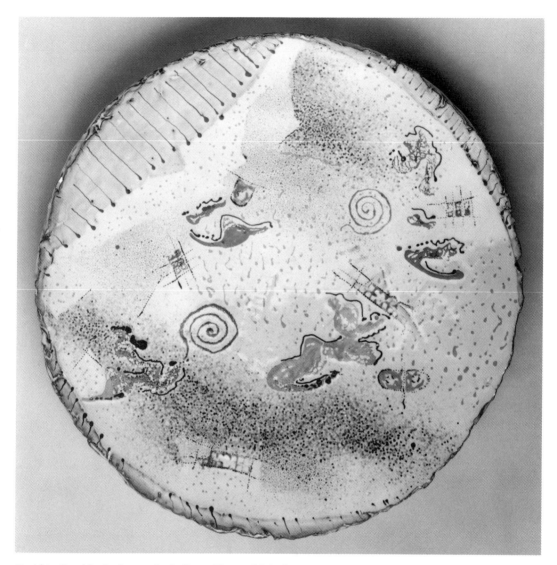

David L. Gamble. Indianapolis, Indiana. Platter, 25 inches.

Gamble uses a many low-fire materials including slips, glaze pencils, glaze crayons, and finishing under-glazes. Cone 05.

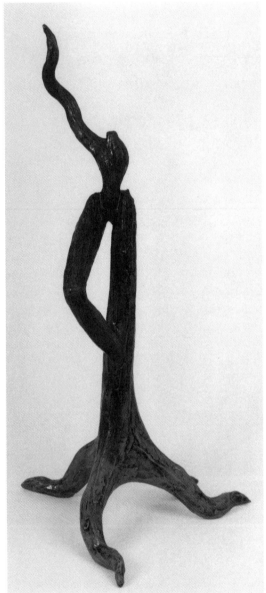

Martha Holt. Tionesta, Pennsylvania. LEFT: "Arbor Vitae," 26 × 20 × 18 inches. RIGHT: "Reach," 39 × 21 × 21 inches. Photos by M. A. Holt.

Holt uses finishing underglazes, glaze crayons, and glaze pencils covered with a clear glaze. She bisque-fires her work to cone 04 and uses a cone 08 final fire.

Richard Zakin. Oswego, New York. ''Painted Tile,'' 15 × 16 cm. Photo by T. C. Eckersley.

A piece painted in a watercolor technique using a finishing underglaze.

LUSTERS

Itsue Ito. Miyazaki, Japan. "So Shu," 25 × 25 × 20 cm.

To make this piece Itsue Ito used multiple layers of painted, airbrushed, and knife-applied glazes and lusters. She fires her pieces to 1040°C (cone 05/04) and uses lower temperatures for the luster firings.

Sally Gaynor. Santa Cruz, California. "Droughtbuster" (teapot), 10 × 10 × 5 inches. Courtesy Winfield Gallery, Carmel, California. Photo by Lee Hocker.

In this piece Gaynor used lusters over commercial glazes,. The piece is fired to cone 06 and then to a lower temperature (cone 019) for the lusters.

Antonella Cimatti. Faenza, Italy. TOP: "Centrotavola," 25 × 25 cm. BELOW: "Vaso," 45 cm high.

Cimatti uses lusters to create her highly painted imagery. She fires her pieces to 950°C (cone 08) and the lusters to 700°C (cone 018).

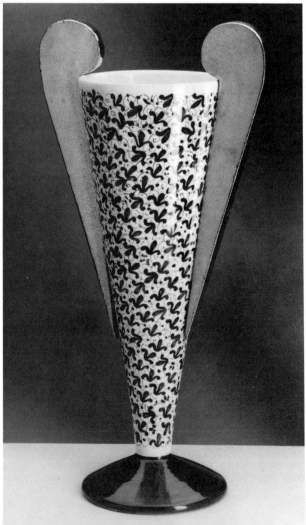

TESTING AND EVALUATION

TEST TILES AND TEST PIECES

The best way to test a ceramic recipe or an image-creation strategy is to try it first on a test tile and then on a test piece. It is especially important that the test tiles you make mirror the character of the work. In addition, always use the same clay body for test pieces that you use in the normal course of your work. If you apply your glazes to ware fired to a low-fire bisque (cones 08 to 04), as most contemporary ceramists do, follow this practice on your test wares as well.

It is a good idea to use the same forming methods to create your test pieces as you use in your work. If most of your work is slab formed, make your tiles from slabs. If you throw most of your work on the potter's wheel, make the tile from a section of a thrown piece and make test pieces on the wheel. I would even recommend that coil builders build their tiles and test pieces using coil-forming methods. Finally, if you add surface imagery to your work, apply surface imagery on at least part of the test piece.

Labeling

If you want to fire more than one test, label each one to avoid confusion. Scratch an identifier into the raw or bisque-fired clay, or label it with a glaze pencil or a solution of water and slip clay or iron oxide.

Test Pieces

Test pieces need not be as large as your normal work, but I make mine large enough to give me an idea of the character of the glaze after firing (Figs. 5-1, 5-2). I usually make test pieces whose dimensions add up to about 100 square centimeters.

Test Tiles

A test body tile must be made from clay that has the same moisture content as clay used for hand-building or throwing. The test tile in Figure 5-3 is about 0.5 centimeters thick, 4 centimeters wide, and 14 centimeters long. To test the tile, inscribe a line 10 centimeters long in the center and make a hole for hanging the tile as shown. Prop up the tile on two pieces of refractory material (pieces of clay or broken kiln shelf) before firing. This will show you if the clay will slump in the fire. A little slumping is to be expected, but if the clay warps too much, it will be difficult to work with. After firing, measure the line again. The line will have shrunk, indicating the shrinkage of the clay body.

Figure 5-4 shows a tile used in glaze testing. This tile should be fairly large—10 to 12 centimeters high—and curved in such a way as to stand in the kiln without support. The surface of the tile should be similar to the surface of your work.

TESTING RECIPES AND IMAGE-CREATION STRATEGIES

Testing and experimentation can be an enjoyable part of ceramics. You have little to lose: if the results are disappointing, you have only lost a test tile and a few minutes of your time. If they are good, you may have gained a great deal.

5-1. Angelo di Petta. Toronto, Canada. Test piece, 4 inches, fired to cone 06.

This sort of test can be used as a final step before applying an experimental glaze to a piece that you value.

5-2. Richard Zakin. Oswego, New York. Photo by T. C. Eckersley.

These test pieces, all approximately 11 cm. high, were used to test the cone 3 glazes that appear in the recipe section of this book.

Testing a Recipe

To test a slip or glaze recipe, you will need:

- Two plastic buckets
- A rubber scraper
- A gram scale
- A 50- or 80-mesh rustproof sieve

The usual amount of a glaze to make up for testing is 100 grams. If you try to test with fewer than 100 grams, your measurements may be inaccurate. Furthermore, most recipes are written so that, aside from the colorants, they add up to 100 grams and need no conversion.

Mixing the Test Glaze

1 While working with dry materials, put on protective clothing and a safety mask approved for use with fine-particle dust.

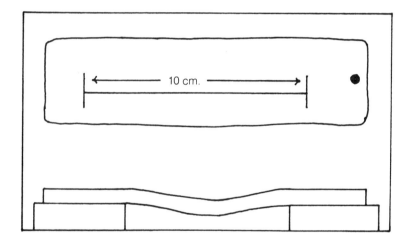

5-3. A test body tile.

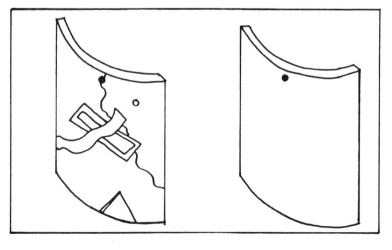

5-4. A glaze testing tile.

2   Weigh the materials.

3   Place the materials as they are weighed in a mixing container.

4   Add water and stir the mixture thoroughly.

5   Place a sieve on top of a second mixing container and pour the test mixture through the sieve into the container.

6   Label the glaze containers carefully.

7   Use a test tile made from a known clay body. (Never test an unknown clay body and an unknown glaze together; always test an unknown with a known.)

8   Apply the glaze to the tile.

9   Label the tile either with a glaze pencil or an iron oxide solution.

If the glaze test looks promising, try it on a larger form. Use it on a piece that is typical of your work and apply it using your normal application methods.

EVALUATING CERAMIC RECIPES

Glaze Attributes

How do you know what to look for when evaluating glaze recipes? To make appropriate choices, you must understand both your own needs and the complex character of glazes. Glazes have a wide range of attributes. In many cases the attribute is clearly revealed after a normal application and firing. In other cases, however, the attribute is not immediately apparent. In these cases I include ways to test for them.

Visual Attributes

Color.   Test for color response by adding various colorants or stains to the base glaze.

Surface (dry, mat, satin mat, satin, satin shiny, shiny, and glossy).   Test for the glaze surface by firing the glaze on your normal clay body in a normal manner. Do remember, however, that if you change the clay body, the glaze surface may change as well.

Visual Texture.   Test for visual texture by applying the glaze in layers of different thicknesses (some recipes are always textured, while others show more texture at a specific thickness).

Light Transmission.   Test for opacity, translucency, or transparency by applying the glaze to test tiles of a different color. An opaque glaze will look the same on both light and dark tiles; a translucent glaze will reveal the color of the tile, but its color will be somewhat obscured; and a transparent glaze will fully (or almost fully) reveal the color of the tile.

Physical Attributes

Durability. To test for durability, which is the ability to withstand abrasion associated with use, scratch the surface of the glaze with a stainless-steel knife. If the knife slides smoothly over the glaze and leaves no mark, it is a durable glaze.

Crawling. To test a high-clay glaze for crawling, apply it in a thick coating to a test tile and fire it in your normal manner. After firing, inspect the surface of the glaze for fissures and cracks.

Crazing. Test for crazing by applying a thick application and rubbing ink over the glaze after firing; the ink will emphasize the thin craze lines. Examine the surface under powerful magnification (use a ten- to twenty-five-power magnifier).

Shivering. Look for signs of buckling, especially at the sharp edges of the form. Magnification may help reveal buckling not visible to the naked eye.

Glaze Flow. Test for glaze flow by placing a generous amount of glaze at the top of a test tile placed vertically in the kiln. Place the tile on a piece of broken kiln shelf in case the glaze runs excessively.

Subjective Judgments

We judge the aesthetic character of a glaze by interpreting its visual and physical attributes. How we judge the aesthetic qualities lies at the very heart of our craft.

I find it useful to differentiate glazes according to their suitability for various tasks. Ceramists whose work is decorative or who make ceramic sculpture make their glaze choices on the basis of aesthetic appeal. Utilitarian potters, who make tableware, planters, or architectural tiles, consider the practical as well as the aesthetic in choosing their glazes.

CHAPTER SIX

CERAMIC GLAZE RECIPES

Ceramists will take great pains to find new and different glaze recipes that will expand the range and enhance the beauty of their work. There are myriad recipes for slips and glazes and each produces a different and in some way unique result.

I have created the recipes in this chapter for those ceramists who wish to make some or all of their slips and glazes in their own studios. During the last year I created and tested perhaps four hundred recipes. I winnowed this number down to the present group, selecting recipes that would be appealing, reliable, durable, stable, and nonrunning. None contains arcane materials, and I have tried to avoid toxic materials as well. A few contain strontium carbonate, a compound not used much until recently, which some see as a useful substitute for barium carbonate.

I have tried to assemble a varied group of recipes so that most ceramists will find at least a few that are of particular appeal. This group of slips and glazes has been created for the firing temperatures of cones 04, 02, 3, 6, and 9.

Following standard practice all recipes total 100 percent (minus colorants).

Note: Ceramists working outside North America will want to look at Appendix A, Materials Availability.

CONE 04 GLAZE RECIPES

Taberg 1

silica	12	Gerstley borate	28
boron frit	50	titanium	2
ball clay	6	zinc	2

Color: with copper carbonate 2, a rich emerald green; with no colorant, a soft milky white
Surface: soft and waxy
Light transmission: translucent (milky opaque where thick)

Visual texture: some in the recipe containing copper (the green is dark where thick)
Durability: excellent

I would characterize this surface as excellent, especially in its color. The surface is easily cleaned and extremely durable. Because it contains no toxic materials, it would be an excellent liner glaze.

Oak Beach 1

silica	10		Gerstley borate	14
spodumene	12		titanium	4
boron frit	40		zirconium	14
kaolin	6			

Color: ivory white
Surface: shiny satin
Light transmission: translucent

Visual texture: none
Durability: excellent

Though this glaze is smooth and enamel-like, it is quite appealing. The soft color is perhaps its most interesting feature.

Straw Yellow

silica	12		red clay	20
soda feldspar	16		Gerstley borate	30
boron frit	22			

Color: light Naples yellow
Surface: satin shiny
Light transmission: opaque (except where thin)

Visual texture: almost none
Durability: excellent

This glaze is interesting because it derives its color from the iron in the red clay. It is at its best when applied in a thick coating, which results in a rich color and surface.

Ohioville

silica	16		red clay	20
spodumene	12		Gerstley borate	20
boron frit	20		zirconium opacifier	12

Color: cream tan
Surface: satin
Light transmission: opaque

Visual texture: a pattern of just-visible red-brown spots (probably derived from the stoneware clay)
Durability: excellent

I would characterize this surface as excellent both in its color and in its "hand."

Tenantville Tan

silica	24		Gerstley borate	20
boron frit	30		zirconium opacifier	8
red clay	18			

Color: ivory
Surface: satin mat where thin; shiny where thick
Light transmission: transparent/translucent

Visual texture: tiny spots that cannot be seen from a distance
Durability: excellent

This surface is excellent, especially when applied in a thin coating, at which point it shows all the clay details.

Ossian Tan

silica	16	Gerstley borate	30
boron frit	24	titanium	2
stoneware clay	18	zirconium opacifier	10

Color: ivory
Surface: shiny
Light transmission: opaque

Visual texture: none
Durability: excellent

This glaze has a simple but serviceable surface; it works best when applied in a fairly thick layer.

Taunton Tan

silica	16	stoneware clay	14
spodumene	10	Gerstley borate	30
boron frit	30		

Color: ivory
Surface: shiny
Light transmission: translucent

Visual texture: none
Durability: excellent

The surface is less shiny than most low-fire transparent/translucent glazes, which makes it unusual. To obtain this effect, soak the kiln (see page 224).

CONE 02 GLAZE RECIPES

Antique Bronze 2

silica	20	Gerstley borate	26
boron frit	44	tin oxide	2
stoneware clay	8	iron	5

Color: burnt sienna
Surface: waxy
Light transmission: translucent

Visual texture: a tight pattern of small dark spots
Durability: excellent

This surface is rich in color and visual texture, and it is extremely durable. While I do not feel that cone 02 pieces should be used to hold food, this glaze will work well for other utilitarian pieces.

Fulton 02–2

soda feldspar	10	Gerstley borate	20
boron frit	46	titanium	2
stoneware clay	12	zirconium opacifier	10

Color: with copper carbonate 2, a bright emer-
ald green; with no colorant, a bright white
Surface: shiny
Light transmission: translucent/transparent

Visual texture: some (dark spots on a lighter
ground)
Durability: excellent

This surface is excellent and one of the best cone 02 glazes in this series. It is durable and should work well for utilitarian pieces.

H.B. Black

silica	20		Gerstley borate	26
boron frit	44		tin oxide	2
stoneware clay	8		iron oxide	18

Color: burnt umber where thin; tobacco brown where thick
Surface: satin shiny
Light transmission: opaque

Visual texture: some; the low viscosity accentuates any texture on the body of the piece
Durability: excellent

The surface of this glaze is rich and dark. The glaze may run, so apply it in a fairly thin layer toward the base of the piece.

Kerryville

soda feldspar	20		stoneware clay	6
boron frit	28		Gerstley borate	16
spodumene	14		titanium	2
Barnard	4		zirconium opacifier	10

Color: butterscotch orange
Surface: satin shiny to shiny
Light transmission: opaque

Visual texture: a great deal; small patterned rutile orange spots
Durability: excellent

The surface of this glaze is excellent, perhaps the best cone 02 glaze in this series. Its appearance is similar to cone 3 and cone 6 glazes. Furthermore, it is quite durable and should work well for utilitarian pieces.

Salter Transparent

boron frit	60		Gerstley borate	18
soda feldspar	12		zinc	2
kaolin	8			

Color: clear
Surface: very shiny
Light transmission: transparent

Visual texture: none
Durability: excellent

This is an excellent transparent glaze—durable, stable, and completely clear.

CONE 3 GLAZE RECIPES

Antique Bronze 1

silica	30		Gerstley borate	26
boron frit	34		tin	2
stoneware clay	8			

Color: with copper carbonate 2 and iron 5, brown to ocher to ocher green; with copper carbonate 2, a cool, clear green
Surface: satin shiny

Visual texture: speckled
Light transmission: little
Durability: excellent

This surface is pleasing because of its excellent color response and visual texture. It is low in alumina, which encourages the rich surface but also causes running. Apply it in a thin layer toward the base of the piece.

Antique Bronze 2

silica	24		stoneware clay	8
boron frit	32		tin	2
Gerstley borate	22		zirconium opacifier	12
copper carbonate	2		iron oxide	5

Color: amber where thin; a warm brown
  where thick
Surface: satin shiny

Visual texture: strong
Light transmission: opaque
Durability: excellent

This complex glaze has interesting color variations and a broken texture. Like Antique Bronze 1, it is low in alumina, which encourages both the rich surface and the glaze's tendency to run toward the base of the piece. Apply it in a thin layer.

April Tan 2

silica	28		Gerstley borate	26
boron frit	36		tin	2
ball clay	8		iron oxide	6

Color: a rich brown
Surface: satin shiny
Visual texture: strong

Light transmission: opaque
Durability: excellent

This surface is quite rich. Most of the clay in the glaze is the dark, high-iron Barnard, from which the glaze derives its dark color and strong visual texture. Because this glaze tends to settle, you may want to add a half percent macaloid (a colloidal material that encourages the glaze components to remain in suspension).

Cadwells Base

soda feldspar	40		strontium	10
boron frit	20		titanium	2
stoneware clay	8		zirconium opacifier	12
dolomite	8		copper carbonate	2

Color: copper aqua
Surface: mat/satin mat
Visual texture: some mottling

Light transmission: opaque
Durability: very good

The dry mat surface of this glaze is reserved. The color is a cool, somewhat muted green. This glaze is at its best when used with other glazes.

Egypt Amber

silica	17		red clay	24
boron frit	34		dolomite	6
soda feldspar	17		titanium	2
iron oxide	6		copper carbonate	2

Color: tan to deep brown to umber
Surface: satin shiny
Visual texture: a tight, small pattern

Light transmission: translucent
Durability: excellent

This appealing glaze has good color and a rich, subtle visual texture.

Dewitt Mills

soda feldspar	10	Barnard	8
boron frit	24	dolomite	16
spodumene	20	zirconium opacifier	12
stoneware clay	8	titanium	2

Color: cream to tan (thick application encourages the cream color)
Surface: satin mat

Visual texture: yes
Light transmission: opaque
Durability: excellent

This surface is rich and appealing, with a good "hand" and lots of visual texture.

Dewitt White 1

soda feldspar	10	dolomite	16
spodumene	20	tin	2
boron frit	24	zirconium opacifier	12
stoneware clay	16		

Color: oyster white
Surface: satin mat
Visual texture: none

Light transmission: opaque
Durability: very good

This glaze is an excellent soft white. By itself it has great appeal, but it also works extremely well with other glazes and colorants. I would characterize it as one of the best recipes in this cone 3 series.

Fulton 4a Deep Blue

boron frit	28	strontium	22
soda feldspar	26	titanium	2
stoneware clay	12	zirconium opacifier	10
iron oxide	6	cobalt oxide	2

Color: gray where thin; deep slate blue where thick
Surface: waxy mat

Visual texture: none
Light transmission: opaque
Durability: excellent

This recipe is appealing in its earthy quality and its soft, waxy mat surface. Its high strontium content may encourage settling.

H.B. Black

silica	30	Gerstley borate	26
boron frit	34	iron oxide	18
stoneware clay	8	tin oxide	2

Color: with copper carbonate 2, a deep umber;
  with cobalt oxide 2, black
Surface: satin shiny

Visual texture: none
Light transmission: opaque
Durability: excellent

The surface of this durable glaze is complex and unusually rich. Because it is low in alumina, it can run excessively. To lessen the chance of running, apply the glaze in a thin layer toward the base of the piece.

K'kat 4

boron frit	28	dolomite	10
spodumene	15	Gerstley borate	10
Barnard	5	titanium	2
stoneware clay	5	zirconium opacifier	25

Color: amber where thin; greenish cream
  where thick
Surface: satin

Visual texture: strongly marked
Light transmission: opaque
Durability: good

This surface is appealing, especially in its warm color and rich dappled texture. The glaze is unusually high in zirconium, which encourages a mat surface while not compromising safety or stability.

Oz Strontium 6

boron frit	26	dolomite	10
spodumene	22	strontium	32
stoneware clay	8	titanium	2
copper carbonate	3		

Color: strong green
Surface: velvet mat
Visual texture: none

Light transmission: opaque
Durability: very good

This recipe is extremely rich and one of the best in this cone 3 series. Its strong points are its visual texture, color, and surface. The surface is similar to a high-barium glaze but does not have the toxicity of barium. It derives these characteristics from its high strontium content. Because of its high strontium content, however, glaze may sediment.

Richmond Mills

soda feldspar	30	stoneware clay	20
boron frit	30	iron	1
talc	11	zirconium opacifier	8

Color: light amber where thin; soft cream
  where thick
Surface: satin mat

Visual texture: tiny oatmeal spots
Light transmission: opaque
Durability: excellent

This glaze has an appealing surface in color and in its "hand." The surface is easily cleaned and extremely durable. Therefore it would be an excellent glaze for application on surfaces in contact with food.

Salter 2 Transparent

soda frit	42	Gerstley borate	18
soda feldspar	30	zinc	2
ball clay	8		

Color: clear
Surface: shiny
Visual texture: none

Light transmission: transparent
Durability: excellent

This fine transparent glaze is durable and appears to be free of crazing (though it is marked with an occasional small bubble). The surface is easily cleaned and durable; it would be an excellent glaze for surfaces in contact with food.

Snyders 2

boron frit	50	stoneware clay	20
soda feldspar	22	zirconium opacifier	8
iron oxide	2		

Color: silver-gray ocher
Surface: shiny satin
Visual texture: highly mottled

Light transmission: opaque
Durability: excellent

The surface of this glaze is very rich. Strong visual textures are revealed when other glazes (especially dark-colored glazes) are applied over it. However, unlike many rich glazes, it is also practical; its surface is easily cleaned and extremely durable. Therefore it would be an excellent glaze for surfaces in contact with food.

Sodus Point 2

boron frit	24	stoneware clay	8
spodumene	24	dolomite	26
Barnard	8	zirconium opacifier	10

Color: yellow ocher and brown
Surface: mat
Visual texture: fairly strong

Light transmission: opaque
Durability: fair

The surface of this glaze is extremely rich, and I feel it is one of the richest glazes in this series of cone 3 recipes. It derives its color from its Barnard/stoneware clay content.

CONE 6 GLAZE RECIPES

Minetto Transparent

silica	10	kaolin	30
boron frit	50	Gerstley borate	10

Color: clear
Surface: a waxy shine
Visual texture: none

Light transmission: translucent
Durability: excellent

I would characterize this surface as rich and highly practical. The surface is easily cleaned and extremely durable. Therefore it would be an excellent glaze for surfaces in contact with food.

Mexico Point Green

soda feldspar	34	dolomite	14
spodumene	14	Gerstley borate	12
kaolin	6	zirconium opacifier	20
		copper carbonate	2.5

Color: soft mossy green
Surface: shiny
Light transmission: opaque

Visual texture: strong
Durability: very durable

This glaze has great appeal, due in large part to its soft, opaque mat surface.

Clear N Base

silica	18	ball clay	12
soda feldspar	40	Gerstley borate	16
wollastonite	10	zinc	4

Color: clear
Surface: glassy
Visual texture: none

Light transmission: transparent
Durability: excellent

This glaze is highly transparent and its surface is shiny and extremely durable. Therefore it would be an excellent glaze for surfaces in contact with food.

Warm Gray Tan 1

boron frit	10	Gerstley borate	18
soda feldspar	36	zirconium opacifier	20
red clay	16		

Color: taupe
Surface: satin shiny
Light transmission: opaque

Visual texture: some soft breakup patterns
Durability: strong

Because of its red clay content, this glaze has a pleasing warm color. Its surface is shiny and extremely durable. Therefore it would be an excellent glaze for surfaces in contact with food.

Denton

soda feldspar	30	kaolin	10
spodumene	12	zirconium opacifier	18
wollastonite	30	copper carbonate	2.5

Color: a cool green
Surface: satin shiny
Light transmission: opaque

Visual texture: none
Durability: very good

The soft-looking surface of this glaze has great appeal, and I would characterize it as very pleasing. It takes color well.

Soft Tan Base

soda feldspar	40	dolomite	14
spodumene	14	zirconium opacifier	22
ball clay	10		

Color: ivory
Surface: mat
Light transmission: opaque

Visual texture: strong
Durability: good

This unusually rich glaze has a soft, warm-looking surface marked by strong glaze-flow patterns.

Satin White

soda feldspar	18	kaolin	10
soda frit	20	dolomite	14
spodumene	14	zirconium opacifier	24

Color: white
Surface: satin mat
Light transmission: opaque

Visual texture: none
Durability: very good

The silver-white opaque surface of this glaze makes it very appealing.

K17

silica	8	dolomite	10
soda feldspar	46	Gerstley borate	10
spodumene	10	zinc	4
kaolin	12	copper carbonate	2.5

Color: soft green
Surface: shiny
Light transmission: transparent

Visual texture: none
Durability: excellent

The rich surface of this glaze is shiny, easily cleaned, and extremely durable. Therefore it would be an excellent glaze for surfaces in contact with food.

New Tyler Amber

soda frit	20	Gerstley borate	20
red clay	60		

Color: deep brown with light-colored spots
Surface: shiny
Light transmission: translucent

Visual texture: strong
Durability: excellent

This simple three-material recipe works well and is extremely durable. Therefore it would be an excellent glaze for surfaces in contact with food.

Pharsalia

soda feldspar	30		red clay	20
spodumene	12		dolomite	18
ball clay	10		Gerstley borate	10

Color: gray ocher
Surface: satin mat
Light transmission: transparent

Visual texture: strongly marked
Durability: excellent

I would characterize this glaze as very rich because of its soft-looking surface and strong visual texture.

Phoenix 2

soda feldspar	30		Barnard	20
ball clay	20		Gerstley borate	30

Color: dark brown
Surface: extremely shiny
Light transmission: transparent

Visual texture: a small pattern of light and dark
Durability: excellent

This glaze has fairly strong appeal in part because of its rich, dark color, which is derived from the Barnard clay. This glaze, with its easily cleaned and durable surface, would be a good glaze for surfaces in contact with food.

TMH 2

soda feldspar	34		Gerstley borate	16
wollastonite	20		zirconium opacifier	20
ball clay	10		cobalt oxide	2

Color: royal blue
Surface: satin shiny
Light transmission: opaque

Visual texture: none
Durability: excellent

This simple, smooth, enamel-like surface does not have the florid character of some glazes, but it looks good, is useful, and takes color very well. The surface of this glaze is shiny and extremely durable. Because it contains no toxic materials, it would be an excellent liner glaze.

TMH 4

soda feldspar	46		Gerstley borate	8
wollastonite	10		zirconium opacifier	18
ball clay	18		cobalt oxide	2

Color: royal blue
Surface: satin mat
Light transmission: opaque

Visual texture: none
Durability: very good

The satin mat surface of this rich glaze derives from the high zirconium content. The surface is reminiscent of a high-barium recipe, though its color responses are different from barium glazes.

Victor Base

soda feldspar	44	Gerstley borate	12
ball clay	6	zirconium opacifier	26
dolomite	12		

Color: white
Surface: satin
Light transmission: opaque

Visual texture: none
Durability: very good

The surface of this glaze is shiny and extremely durable. It would be an excellent glaze for application on surfaces which come into contact with food. Many utilitarian potters like to use a white glaze for this purpose because food looks so attractive on a white background.

Transparent Mat Glaze

boron frit	30	ball clay	40
wollastonite	25	dolomite	5

Color: clear
Surface: mat to satin mat
Light transmission: translucent

Visual texture: none
Durability: excellent

This rich glaze is unusual in that it is a transparent mat glaze. This interesting, useful glaze type was popular in the United States from the early 1900s to the 1930s. Glazes of this sort must be fired with a long soaking period (see page 224).

Wollbase 4

soda frit	10	red clay	24
wollastonite	40	Gerstley borate	6
ball clay	20		

Color: ocher
Surface: shiny
Light transmission: transparent

Visual texture: none
Durability: very good

The color of this glaze has a pleasing warmth. Its surface is shiny, easily cleaned, and extremely durable. It contains no toxic materials and therefore would be an excellent glaze for surfaces which come into contact with food.

Metalblack

Barnard	90	Gerstley borate	10
		copper carbonate	6

Color: umber black
Surface: satin shiny
Light transmission: opaque

Visual texture: none
Durability: good

This gun-metal glaze has an interesting metallic black surface, but it is somewhat drier in surface effect than most glazes of its type.

CONE 9 GLAZE RECIPES

Allen Creek Base 92

potash feldspar	50	dolomite	30
ball clay	10	Gerstley borate	10

Color: white
Surface: satin mat
Light transmission: translucent where thin; opaque where thick

Visual texture: strong textures derived from calcium and magnesium
Durability: very good

I would characterize this surface as rich.

Ridgebury

silica	10	dolomite	18
spodumene	12	red clay	30
wollastonite	30		

Color: iron green to orange
Surface: satin shiny
Light transmission: transparent

Visual texture: strong texture derived from lithium, calcium, and titanium
Durability: fair

The surface of this glaze is rich but a bit unstable and crazed where thick. The glaze seems to work best when applied over other glazes to encourage visual texture.

Conquest R 92

spodumene	10	dolomite	6
soda feldspar	20	Gerstley borate	20
red clay	44		

Color: burnt umber
Surface: very shiny
Light transmission: transparent

Visual texture: strong texture derived from lithium, calcium, and titanium
Durability: excellent

The surface of this glaze is fairly rich, easily cleaned, and extremely durable. Therefore it would be an excellent glaze for surfaces in contact with food.

Franklin R 92

silica	8	red clay	22
potash feldspar	32	dolomite	30
ball clay	8	iron	8

Color: red brown to burnt umber
Surface: satin
Light transmission: opaque

Visual texture: strong texture derived from iron and calcium/magnesium
Durability: excellent

This is one of my favorite glazes of the cone 9 group. Its surface is extremely rich.

Gateville R 92

dolomite	30	potash feldspar	20
red clay	40	spodumene	10

James L. Tanner. Janesville, Minnesota. "Dreamer," 22½ × 16½ × 3 inches.

In his work Tanner has taken the ancient technique of slip trailing and extended it to create a new kind of imagery which is very much his own. He fires his work to cone 04 and cone 019.

Richard Burkett. San Diego, California. "Red Top," 11 × 10 × 4 inches.

This is a porcelain piece fired to cone 6, finished with cone 6 glazes and cone 06 overglazes. Dense white porcelain is effectively combined with brilliant, low-fire color.

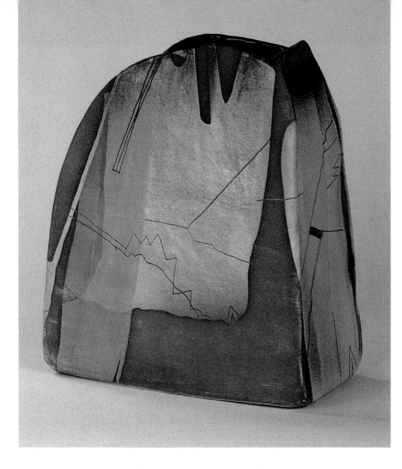

Richard Zakin. Oswego, New York. Vase, 26 × 24 × 11.5 cm. Photo by T.C. Eckersley.

An exploration of surface creation strategies. A green terra sigillata was applied first, then lighter-colored glazes. Next sgraffito imagery was drawn into the surface of the glazes. Finally, a dark-colored glaze was sprayed at the top of the piece. Cone 3.

Giovanni Cimatti. Faenza, Italy. "Ecologica."

Cimatti uses stained engobes and sgraffito to create his richly textured surfaces. He fires his work to 980–1000°C (cone 07–06).

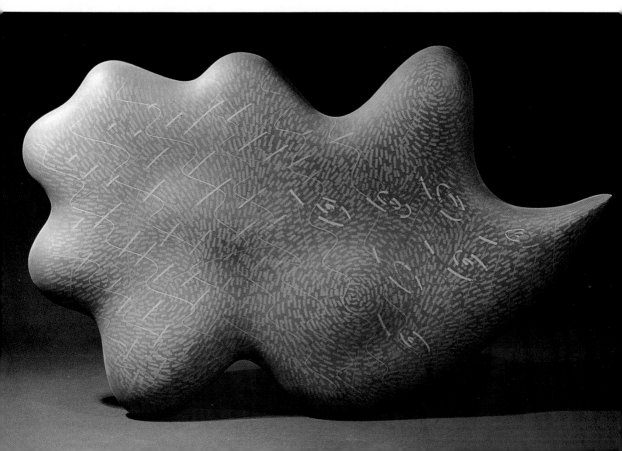

Ann Mortimer. New Market, Ontario, Canada. "Walled Skyscape," 43 × 38 × 1.5 cm.

This piece has a strongly illusionistic and painterly quality. It was finished with glazes and fired to cone 04 with "room temperature" (artist's paint) highlights applied after firing.

David Gamble. Indianapolis, Indiana. Platter, 27 inches (diameter).

Gamble has introduced many studio artists to the possibilities of commercially prepared underglazes and glazes. Cone 05.

Richard Notkin. Myrtle Point, Oregon.
"Cube Skull Teapot: (Variation #19),"
Yixing Series, $8 \frac{5}{8} \times 6 \frac{3}{4} \times 3$ inches.
Courtesy of Garth Clark Gallery, New
York and Los Angeles. Photo by R.
Notkin.

*Notkin uses unglazed surfaces to
heighten the effect of his highly carved
imagery. Cone 5–6.*

Victor Spinski. Newark, Delaware. "I
Am Giving Away My Tools. . . . Just
Bought a New Computer," $8 \frac{3}{4} \times 15 \times 11 \frac{1}{2}$ inches. Photo by Butch Hullet.

*Spinski depicts everyday objects in an
ironic way. He fires his glazes to cone
04; decals and luster glazes are fired to
cone 018.*

William Stewart. Hamlin, New York.
"Fork," $81 \times 20 \times 10$ inches.

*Stewart uses brush application and
sgraffito techniques to create a very
personal imagery. Cone 04/03.*

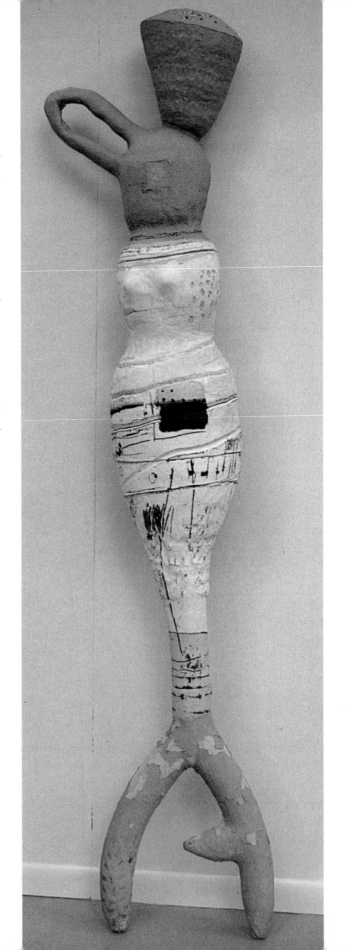

Donna Nicholas. Edinboro, Pennsylvania. "Gyre XI," 30 × 38 × 9 inches. Photo by Howard Goldsmith.

Nicholas's reserved use of brilliant color results in a piece whose color and form work together to create a sense of unity. Cone 04.

John Stephenson. Ann Arbor, Michigan "Twisted Earthscape #22," 22³⁄₄ × 22 × 32¹⁄₂ inches. Photo by Suzanne Coles.

Using thick applications of colored slips, finished with a coating of a clear glaze, John Stephenson creates brilliant color that is in no way ingratiating. Cone 03.

Color: ocher to amber to dark brown
Surface: satin
Light transmission: translucent where thin; opaque where thick

Visual texture: strong texture derived from lithium, calcium/magnesium, and titanium
Durability: excellent

The surface of this glaze is rich with a strong visual texture.

Gateville Stone 92

soda feldspar	30	dolomite	20
spodumene	10	Gerstley borate	10
stoneware	30		

Color: oatmeal
Surface: satin mat
Light transmission: opaque

Visual texture: strong texture (brown dots in a cream field) derived from lithium, calcium/magnesium, and titanium
Durability: excellent

The surface of this glaze is rich and its mat surface and small, dark-colored spots give it an appealing stony quality.

H GK 92

soda feldspar	44	dolomite	18
spodumene	16	zirconium	14
kaolin	8		

Color: bone white
Surface: stony/dry and pitted
Light transmission: opaque

Visual texture: none
Durability: fair

The surface of this glaze is strong rather than beautiful. There is a good deal of interest in glazes with "nonstandard surfaces" at present, and this glaze fits into this category. It works well by itself and with other glazes.

Harpersfield R 92

spodumene	10	red clay	44
ball clay	16	dolomite	30
iron	8		

Color: red brown
Surface: satin
Light transmission: opaque

Visual texture: strong
Durability: good

This glaze is unstable and bubbling when thickly applied. When applied in a normal coating, the surface is rich with a very appealing color.

Deerpark Base

silica	10	red clay	18
spodumene	8	dolomite	34
ball clay	30		

Color: amber cream to amber
Surface: satin mat glaze
Light transmission: translucent

Visual texture: strong texture derived from iron and calcium/magnesium
Durability: excellent

The surface of this glaze is excellent. It is easily cleaned and extremely durable. Therefore it would be an excellent glaze for surfaces which come into contact with food.

Pilgrim Vitreous Engobe 92

potash feldspar	12	Gerstley borate	2
talc	20	tin	2
ball clay	52	zirconium	12

Color: white
Surface: semivitreous with a slight sheen
Light transmission: opaque

Visual texture: some
Durability: excellent

The surface of this glaze is very appealing and works well with other glazes. It is also quite durable.

Shan 92

spodumene	10	dolomite	24
ball clay	18	Gerstley borate	12
red clay	36		

Color: ocher to amber brown
Surface: satin shiny
Light transmission: translucent where thin; opaque where thick

Visual texture: strong texture derived from lithium, iron, and calcium/magnesium
Durability: excellent

The surface of this glaze is very rich, easily cleaned, and extremely durable. Therefore it would be an excellent glaze for surfaces which come into contact with food.

Woodbourne Base 92

soda feldspar	44	ball clay	8
red clay	20	dolomite	28

Color: amber yellow
Surface: satin mat
Light transmission: opaque

Visual texture: very little
Durability: excellent

The surface of this glaze is excellent and quite stable. It is easily cleaned and extremely durable. Therefore it would be an excellent glaze for surfaces which come into contact with food.

CHAPTER SEVEN

CREATING IMAGERY

For many ceramists (and I include myself), creating the surface of the piece is the most exciting and demanding part of the ceramic process. I feel this is particularly true because I fire in oxidation. My approach to firing in the oxidation atmosphere requires that I take imaginative approaches to the creation of the surface finish.

In this chapter I will discuss strategies for creating rich and personal surfaces suitable for oxidation work at various firing temperatures. Particularly interesting to me are the complex strategies many ceramists employ which allow them to build a surface using various materials and application methods in concert.

CREATING IMAGERY IN CLAY

When we are asked to think about creating a rich, personal surface on our pieces, we turn naturally to thoughts of glazes and similar surface treatments. However, many ceramists begin the process of creating surface imagery by manipulating the clay itself. These manipulations may be additive, subtractive, or molded. Our clay surfaces can be (1) sprigged or inlaid (additive), (2) carved, gouged, combed, engraved, or stamped (subtractive), or (3) textured or press-formed (molded). In Figure 7-1 we see now a stamped image can be used to create imagery.

When slips or glazes are applied over such manipulated surfaces their appearance is often significantly enhanced, and a unity is created between form to surface. The techniques required to accomplish these results are usually simple and direct. They also can be very personal and exciting, as can be seen in the Imagery in Clay photos beginning on page 147.

CLAY INLAY

In recent years ceramists working in a contemporary vein have engaged in explorations of clay inlay techniques. Though there are many possible variations of the technique, the underlying principle remains the same: a clay of one color is placed next to a clay of another color.

Clay inlay requires experiment and testing because a clay that shrinks a great deal may not be compatible with one that shrinks only a little. The results, however, can be very rich. The photos in the Clay Inlay and Colored Porcelain series begin on page 156.

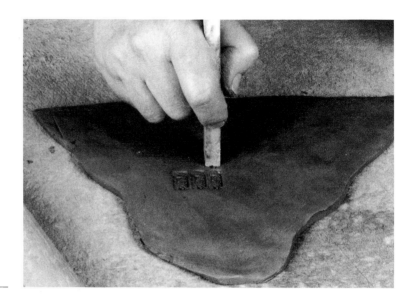

7-1. Creating imagery in clay. Photo by T. C. Eckersley.

APPLICATION OF OXIDATION SURFACES

The skills needed to apply a surface finish to ceramic work successfully are complex and demanding. Many of these skills require a good deal of practice before they can be mastered. Remember that whenever you try a new method of glaze application, use an expendable practice piece.

The different ways to apply glazes are described below. Photos of pieces glazed in various ways begin on page 162.

Dip Application

Of all the methods of glaze application, dipping is the simplest and most direct. The potter simply dips the object to be glazed into a bucket of liquid stain, slip, engobe, or glaze. Be sure to mix a sufficiently large amount of the recipe beforehand (5,000 to 10,000 grams).

Dip application is accomplished as follows: Hold the object in your fingers or use glaze tongs to grasp the piece. If you hold the object in your hand, grasp one part firmly and lower the piece into the bucket. Allow the piece to dry. Then grasp carefully part of the section already covered and immerse the untreated section of the piece. To make sure the piece is completely covered, the dipped areas must overlap. If the surface covering is a glaze, the overlapped section will look quite different from the rest of the glaze in color and texture; it will be stronger in color and more opaque.

If you wish to use a dip application and yet avoid this overlap, use tongs. Glazing tongs are plier-like devices that enable the potter to dip entire pieces into the bucket in one operation. The tongs will leave tiny marks, which can be filled with a brush. Before using, practice with the tongs and learn to use them correctly. Dip and retrieve the piece smoothly and slowly to avoid drips and runs. If you use them correctly, tongs leave no evidence of their use.

Be careful to grip the piece lightly; if you apply too much pressure, the piece may break. Pieces weighing more than fifteen or twenty pounds are difficult to dip with tongs. Therefore dip large pieces by hand, or apply the glaze using pouring or spraying methods.

Pour and Splash Application

In this method of application, the potter pours or splashes stains, slips, engobes, or glaze over the piece. This method results in a surface modulated by variations in thickness of application. The results are characteristically soft and irregular with a flowing imagery.

You need to prepare only a small amount of the recipe. Place a catch basin below the object and pour the glaze over the object. You may reuse any excess glaze that accumulates in the catch basin.

Brush Application

The ceramist who works with glazes prepared in the studio will rarely apply those glazes with a brush. Studio preparations are rarely mixed in such a way as to work well with a brush. Commercial glazes, which are very finely ground and contain gums and suspension agents, are prepared for brush application and most often are applied with brushes.

Because brushes and brush techniques vary, you will need to do a great deal of experimenting to find out what effects you can achieve when applying stains, slips, engobes, and glazes. The Chinese or Japanese bamboo brush gives a soft, sinuous line. The Japanese hake, a flat, soft-bristle brush, gives a much wider line, which is beautiful when charged with glaze or used in a dry-brush technique. Sign-writer's brushes produce a thin, controlled line. House-painter's brushes (especially old ones) produce an interesting textured effect.

Spray Application

Spraying can be used alone or in conjunction with other application methods. It is often the best method for applying a surface treatment on large pieces that cannot be dipped. You will need to practice before you will become proficient with a sprayer. Layers of glaze applied too quickly and heavily will puddle and drip, creating a messy surface. Furthermore, it is difficult to gauge the thickness of a coating and you will have few clues as to whether an application is too thin or too thick. Finally, the surface of the unfired sprayed piece often smudges easily. In this case adding a small amount of binder (2 percent of a colloidal material is effective) will prevent this from happening. Take care also during loading to avoid smudging. Spraying works well as the final treatment of a piece, used to soften and enrich a dipped or poured application.

Spray Booths.   Spraying naturally releases a good deal of glaze dust into the atmosphere. Spray booths are designed to collect these dusts. They are constructed in the form of a large box. The piece is placed in the box for spraying. Use of a spray booth keeps the dust to a minimum. Generally the dust is exhausted into the open air, where it is dispersed. An alternative is to collect the dust in a flowing sheet of water, but this is too expensive to construct in most studios. Always wear a good dust mask during the spraying process.

External-Mix Sprayers.   The external-mix of sprayer (Fig. 7-2), a simple device with few controls, is particularly suitable for spraying ceramic mixtures and has a number of important advantages. Aside from being inexpensive, it is highly immune to blockages (even when it is used to spray unscreened materials), and easily cleaned. This type of sprayer works on a different principle than most paint sprayers. Unlike other sprayers, in an external-mix sprayer the air from the compressor and the liquid glaze do not mix inside the sprayer but rather at a point midway between the air and glaze nozzles, thus avoiding the weaknesses of most spray mechanisms. Any blockage would occur in the feed tube connected to the glaze container. Because this tube is open and straight, it can be cleaned easily. Nozzles of various sizes are made for external-mix sprayers. A large nozzle can accommodate rough, unscreened mixtures. An external-mix sprayer requires little air—25 p.s.i. (pounds per square inch)—and can be used with almost any compressor.

Masking and Resist Materials

Masking and resist materials allow the ceramist to reserve areas of the surface of the piece so that they are free of slip or glaze. Various materials can be used as masks or resists. The most popular is masking tape. Another is frisket, a latex-based viscous liquid that is painted on parts of the piece.

Masking materials work on the following principle: the ceramist presses the masking material on the surface of the piece and applies the slip or glaze, covering both the surface of

7-2. This simple external mix sprayer is an excellent tool for applying glazes. Courtesy Minnesota Midwest Clay Company. Photo by T. C. Eckersley.

the piece and the masking material. When the masking material is removed, the slip or glaze on the masking material is removed as well. The masking material must stick firmly to the surface of the piece and not loosen even if immersed in the liquid glaze. Once it has served its purpose, it should be easy to remove and should leave no residue that might resist further glaze application.

Resists are waxy or greasy materials that are drawn or painted on the surface of the piece. They resist any slips and glazes applied over them. They can be left on the piece because they will burn away during the firing. Wax is the most popular resist, although fats and resins can be used as well. Water-soluble liquid waxes have been developed especially for ceramists. They are effective, easy to use, and are nonflammable (unlike paraffin, which must be heated for use and which is quite flammable).

Trailing or Tracing

A trailer or tracer is a tool for applying a thick line of slip or glaze to the surface of the ware. They rely in some way on air pressure and are often flexible plastic or rubber bulbs with a narrow nozzle at one end. Other types rely on air blown through a tube by the ceramist. The result is a raised, linear design covering parts of the piece.

PATHS TO RICH GLAZE APPLICATION

Over the centuries ceramists have developed complex strategies for creating ceramic imagery. Ceramic imagery conveys a sense of experimentation and can be used to create highly personal statements.

Painted and Drawn Imagery

A classic way of creating interesting ceramic surfaces is to embellish the surface of the work with painted imagery. This strategy is especially useful in the oxidation fire because painted imagery is more compatible with oxidation's simple, unbroken surfaces. Painting is one of the best ways to create rich and complex surfaces in the oxidation fire.

There are a great many possibilities open to the ceramist who wishes to work with painted imagery. I list a number of these below. Photos of pieces with painted and drawn imagery begin on page 168.

Maiolica.   In maiolica work, the ceramist paints coloring oxides and stains over an opaque, white, or light-colored base glaze. The piece is first immersed in the base glaze, then coloring oxides and stains are painted directly on the surface of the base glaze. These stain the glaze and create the imagery.

While maiolica traditionally required low-fire glazes fluxed with lead, the technique can be used with leadless base glazes at any firing temperature. This is desirable as we no longer wish to use toxic materials such as lead. I have seen effective results from maiolicas fired in the mid-fire range. These modifications produce results that do not exactly duplicate the low-fire, lead-containing maiolica work, but they can be quite rich. In addition, they are more suitable than classical maiolica for utilitarian pieces.

In Figures 7-3 through 7-5 we see a variation on the traditional maiolica technique developed by the sculptor Ann Roberts.

Slip Painting Under a Clear Glaze.   Nonflowing slips are especially useful for painting strategies. Unlike recipes that flow a good deal, these tend to "stay put." They are not marked by the blurring or smearing that marks imagery painted with flowing glazes. These high-clay slips are usually covered with a transparent glaze. The resulting imagery can be quite painterly.

Glaze Painting.   Ceramic imagery can also be created by painting glazes directly on the surface of the piece. Most glazes are inappropriate for this purpose because they flow too much and blur the imagery. The glaze must be stiff and stay in place. Glazes with a clay content over 15 percent are more likely to stay in place.

Binders are often added to glaze recipes to ensure that they flow smoothly and adhere to the surface of the piece. Care must be taken when painting with glazes that the imagery does not get too fussy. Because many glazes do not reveal their true character until they are fired, a surface that looks smooth and well applied may become sloppy upon firing. You must experiment with various techniques and strategies in order to be sure of good results.

Flowing Glazes

The best flowing glazes do not flow so much as to destroy the integrity of the image, but their flow is strong enough to erase evidence of the brushwork and create rich visual textures. The imagery can be quite striking. Be careful that you do not overfire the piece: overfired flowing glazes will often flow excessively.

Sgraffito

Sgraffito methods require the application of a layer of slip, engobe, or glaze; the ceramist then carves through this layer back to the clay body. Sgraffito is characterized by a crisp linear imagery (see the photos beginning on page 191 and Figure 7-13). It is especially of interest to ceramists working in oxidation because it helps the ceramist exploit the possibilities of oxidation firing to the full, using a fluent, graphic imagery.

Two common sgraffito techniques involve (1) the use of a dark slip over a light body and (2) the use of a light slip over a dark body. In both cases the design is scratched through the slip to the body. Apply a light coating of clear glaze as the final coating.

In Figures 7-6 through 7-12 we see the way in which Angelo di Petta uses sgraffito techniques with glazes. In Figure 7-13 we see another use of sgraffito technique with slips used by Eric Mellon.

Intaglio Glazing

In intaglio glazing, the potter daubs glaze into the textured areas of the bisqued piece and then sponges the surface so that the glaze remains only in the interstices (crevices) of the form. Daubing and sponging heighten the contrast between the textured and untextured areas of the piece and enrich its surface. (See the photos beginning on page 194.)

Intaglio glazing is a two-stage process. The ceramist presses, stamps, scratches, or carves the textures into the clay when the piece is formed or soon after. The piece is then bisque-fired and the glaze applied. This method is simple and reliable; furthermore, it is WYSIWYG (what you see is what you get). These characteristics allow even beginning ceramists a great deal of freedom. Both linear imagery and shaded effects can be produced easily using these methods.

While the technique of intaglio glazing can be used alone, it is often done in combination with dipping, splashing, or spraying and combines effectively with them.

Multilayer and Multiapplication Glazing Strategies

In the oxidation fire, a simple application of a single slip or glaze is likely to produce a surface that lacks subtlety and richness. When different glazes are applied, one over another, the complex interactions can produce visually rich, complex surfaces. Photos of pieces made with multiple applications and materials begin on page 201.

Using more than one application method when glazing a piece can produce complex and surprising results because each application method leaves its own particular mark.

Oxidation work can benefit a great deal from complex combinations of multilayer surfaces and applications. While some of these applications may sound time-consuming and demanding, they need not be. Applying two or three different recipes inventively can produce complex, personal imagery. For my vase shown on page 208, I splashed over a painted terra sigillata base and then applied sgraffito imagery.

CREATING COMPLEX IMAGERY

Using well-thought-out methods to apply glazes is perhaps the most important key to mastering electric kiln ceramics. Unless they are manipulated imaginatively, oxidation-fired glazes will not have the visual complexity of glazes fired in fuel-burning reduction kilns. Ceramists working in the oxidation fire can compensate, however, by manipulating glazes in an imaginative manner and employing a wide variety of recipes and application strategies. Using these methods, we too can create rich imagery.

For example, we can use many slips and glazes and multiple glaze colors on the same piece and use them not only next to each other but in multiple layers, one on top of the other, as well. The result can be a complex surface that speaks well of the intermixing of glaze layers in the heat of the fire.

These glaze-application methods are appropriate for both glazes made in the studio and

ANN ROBERTS APPLIES A GLAZE

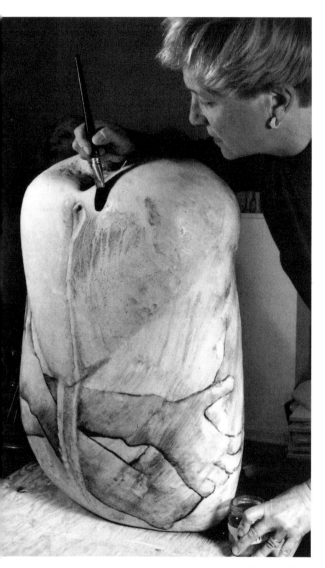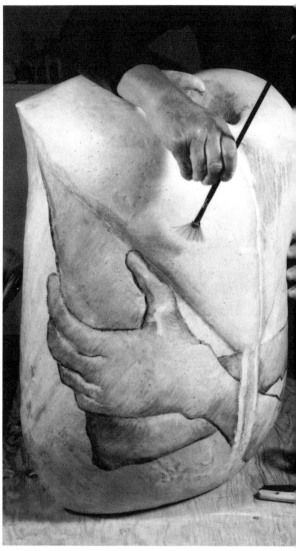

7-3, 7-4. To create her pieces Roberts first applies an opaque mat glaze, which is bisque fired to cone 02. She then brushes stains and coloring oxides over this. These are fired to cone 06. The work can be returned again and again to the fire if desired. It could be said that the artist has created her own variation on the maiolica process—one that is especially suited to the creation of imagery on large ceramic sculpture. Photos by Jeanne Wolfe.

7-5. Ann Roberts. Conestogo, Ontario, Canada. ''Tree of Life, Back to Back,'' 146.5 × 36.8 × 40.7 cm. Photo by Jeanne Wolfe.

A sculptural piece in which Roberts has employed her glaze application strategy.

ANGELO DI PETTA PAINTS A PIECE

7-6. Establishing the drawing. Many of di Petta's design elements are based on sgraffito techniques using a compass.

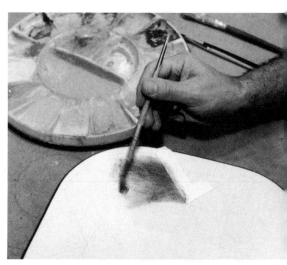

7-7. Painting an area of color using a thin stain (note the use of tape as a mask).

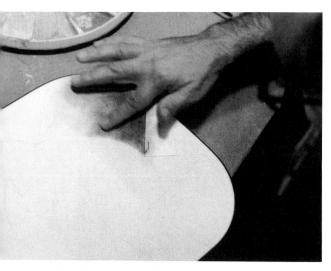

7-8. Di Petta smooths the area of color with his finger.

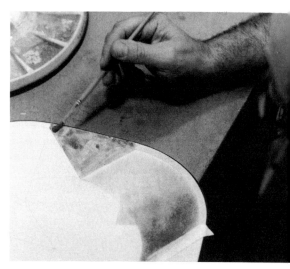

7-9. Painting another color area.

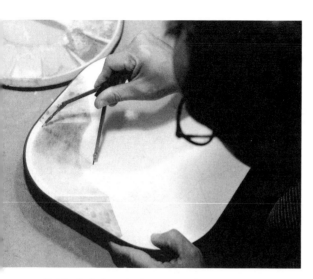

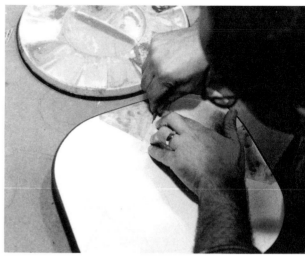

7-10. Refining the imagery using a compass and a needle to create engraved sgraffito lines.

7-11. Continuing the image creation process.

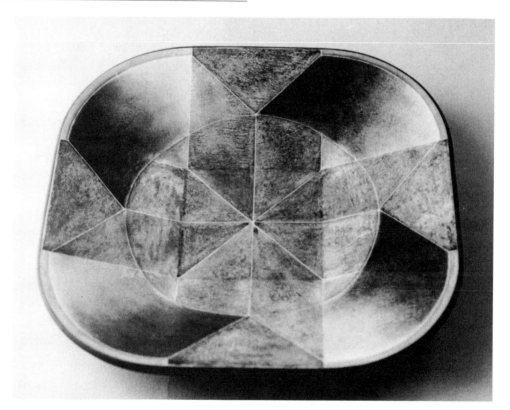

7-12. Angelo di Petta. Toronto, Ontario, Canada. "Painted Plate."

This is an example of the work di Petta creates using these techniques.

7-13. Eric James Mellon (Bognor Regis, England) using a sgraffito technique to decorate a bowl. Photo by Chris Hadow Photography.

commercial glazes. While the glaze strategies require attention and imagination, they need not be time-consuming or difficult. Applying two or three different recipes or implementing two or three application strategies can be accomplished swiftly by the dexterous ceramist.

An impressive example of the creation of a complex glaze application strategy can be seen in the work of Sandra Blaine (page 217) in which organic materials, stains, and glazes are applied while the piece is still wet. The piece is then fired to bisque, more stains and glazes are applied, and the piece is fired once more.

THE INTERACTION OF GLAZES—SIX CONE 3 GLAZES USED WITH EACH OTHER

Knowing how two or more glaze layers interact can help the ceramist determine the effects that will be produced in the oxidation fire. I designed an experiment, shown in the following charts, by choosing a group of six glazes. I applied each glaze in the group to every other glaze, creating thirty-six combinations (including each glaze by itself) to determine the interactions created by each combination.

If you are familiar with glaze-testing procedures, you will note that this procedure is similar to the "line blend" testing procedure, in which two glazes are blended together. In this experiment, however, I layered the glazes rather than blending them and found the resulting effects far more florid and exciting than those I would have obtained by blending.

Note: In each chart I start with a single glaze and then describe the effects of that glaze by itself and then with each other glaze applied over it.

Chart 1. Base Glaze: Antique Bronze 2

Antique Bronze 2
by itself

This is a shiny, highly figured glaze, marked by dark green spots on an emerald green ground.

April Tan 2
over Antique
Bronze 2

This shiny, highly figured combination is marked by a strong glaze flow and green spots on a brown ground.

Dewitt White 1
over Antique
Bronze 2

This combination is marked by a strong glaze flow and some pitting. Its color is a soft emerald green.

Dewitt Mills
over Antique
Bronze 2

The surface of this combination is highly figured. It is marked by light green spots on a tan ground.

Oz Strontium 6
over Antique
Bronze 2

The low viscosity of the Oz Strontium glaze encourages strong glaze flow and a complex visual texture marked by white spots on a dark blue ground. This is a very successful combination.

Richmond Mills
over Antique
Bronze 2

The low viscosity of the Richmondville glaze encourages a highly figured surface with white spots on an emerald green ground.

Chart 2. Base Glaze: April Tan 2

April Tan 2
by itself

This is a shiny, highly figured glaze, marked by tobacco brown spots on an amber ground. This is a rich glaze.

Antique Bronze 2
over April Tan 2

The low viscosity of the Antique Bronze glaze encourages a highly figured surface. It is shiny and marked by brown spots on a soft green ground. This is a rich combination.

Dewitt White 1
over April Tan 2

This combination results in a shiny, highly figured surface with brown spots on a cream ground. It is quite rich.

Dewitt Mills
over April Tan 2

This combination results in a fairly low viscosity. The surface is shiny and tan-amber in color.

Oz Strontium 6
over April Tan 2

The very low viscosity of the Oz Strontium results in shiny, amber patches over watery dark blue. It is a rich combination.

Richmond Mills
over April Tan 2

This combination results in a shiny, very highly figured surface with brown spots on a white ground. It is a rich combination.

Chart 3. Base Glaze: Dewitt White 1

Dewitt White 1
by itself

This is a soft, creamy mat white marked with tiny brown dots. It is rich in surface.

Antique Bronze 2
over Dewitt
White 1

This combination is shiny and bubbly. It is emerald green in color.

April Tan 2
over Dewitt
White 1

This combination is shiny and highly figured, with brown spots on a white ground. Its surface is very rich.

Dewitt Mills over Dewitt White 1	This combination results in a satin mat, highly figured surface with white spots on a tan ground.
Oz Strontium 6 over Dewitt White 1	This combination results in a satin mat, highly figured surface with white spots on a soft, violet-blue ground. It is quite rich.
Richmond Mills over Dewitt White 1	This combination results in a satin, shiny, enamel-like, rich white surface.

Chart 4. Base Glaze: Dewitt Mills

Dewitt Mills by itself	This is a mat surface with figured tan amber spots on a stable brown ground.
Antique Bronze 2 over Dewitt Mills	This combination encourages a bubbly, unstable, surface with highly figured green spots on a brown ground.
April Tan 2 over Dewitt Mills	This combination results in a bubbly, unstable, low-viscosity surface with amber spots on a brown ground. Though marked by stability problems, its surface is very rich.
Dewitt White 1 over Dewitt Mills	This combination encourages a stable surface, with brown-amber spots on a white ground. It is a very rich combination.
Oz Strontium 6 over Dewitt Mills	This combination results in an unstable, highly figured surface with white and dark blue spots on a green-tan ground. Though there are stability problems, this is a rich combination.
Richmond Mills over Dewitt Mills	This is a stable combination with brown spots on a white ground. It is shiny in surface and quite rich.

Chart 5. Base Glaze: Oz Strontium 6

Oz Strontium 6 by itself	This glaze is a dry, barium-like mat blue.
Antique Bronze 2 over Oz Strontium 6	This combination produces a highly figured surface with white spots on a ground which is light tan where thin and dark blue where thick. This is a rich surface.
April Tan 2 over Oz Strontium 6	The low viscosity of these two glazes encourages a watery, dark blue, shiny surface where thick; light tan where thin. This combination is quite rich.
Dewitt White 1 over Oz Strontium 6	This combination produces a low-viscosity, mat surface, light blue in color.
Dewitt Mills over Oz Strontium 6	This combination results in a surface that is mat tan where thick and brown where thin. This is another rich combination.
Richmond Mills over Oz Strontium 6	This combination results in a shiny surface with dark blue spots on a streaky white ground. A rich combination.

Chart 6. Base Glaze: Richmond Mills

Richmond Mills by itself	This is a rich, shiny surface with a smooth, unbroken texture and an ivory color.
Antique Bronze 2 over Richmond Mills	This combination results in a low-viscosity, satin shiny surface, marked by figuration, with green spots on a light green ground. It is a rich combination.
April Tan 2 over Richmond Mills	This combination encourages a shiny, low-viscosity surface with some figuration. It is marked by brown spots on a tan ground.
Dewitt White 1 over Richmond Mills	This combination results in a mat surface with a fairly sparse pattern of tan spots on the ivory ground. This is a very successful combination.
Dewitt Mills over Richmond Mills	This combination produces a satin mat, low-viscosity surface, with reddish spots on a tan ground.
Oz Strontium 6 over Richmond Mills	The low viscosity of the Oz Strontium encourages a wood-ash-like pattern, a satin to satin shiny surface with dark blue patches on a watery blue ground. This is a rich combination.

USING THE ELECTRIC KILN FOR RAKU AND SMOKE-REDUCTION FIRING

A number of ceramists in recent years have experimented with the electric kiln for raku and smoke-reduction firings with some success. See the photos beginning on page 219.

Raku with Postfiring Reduction

Electric-fired raku typically is fired to cone 06/04, at which point the ceramist withdraws the piece from the kiln and places it in a fireproof container filled with combustible materials, such as sawdust or leaves. When the container is sealed, causing smoke reduction, the unglazed areas of the piece turn a soft smoky black and the glaze colors become modified and enriched. While the process can be hard on the kiln and the kiln elements, the results have the same rich color and character of raku fired in a fuel-burning kiln.

The Danish ceramist Nina Höle makes raku in an electric kiln out of necessity: ''Since a kiln is something one has to have, it should be easy to regulate, dependable, trouble-free, and affordable. I consider that bottled gas is unsuitable because my workshop is underground. Natural gas is not available to me as I live in a relatively unpopulated area without natural gas lines. Therefore the electric kiln is the answer for me. Luckily, we have in Denmark the lowest electrical rates in Western Europe.'' Nina Höle's raku is shown on page 222.

Smoke Reduction

Smoke reduction creates a rich, flashed imagery that is very different from the results produced by most electric kiln firings. Though it goes against accepted practice, some ceramists have made a good case for smoke-reduction firing in the electric kiln. The electric kiln in general is not suitable for reduction firing. However, because smoke reduction is a low-fire technique, much less stress is placed on the elements than would be the case if similar techniques were used at higher temperature. With care, the kiln elements will last a long time.

Smoke-reduction firings require the use of a saggar, which is a sealed container placed inside the firing chamber. A bed of flammable material such as sawdust is placed in the base of the saggar and the ware is placed on top. More flammable material is packed around the piece. The saggar is then put into the kiln and fired. As it burns, the sawdust carbonizes the surface of the piece, creating a rich, highly varied surface.

It is easy to see why ceramists might want to enjoy the convenience and flexibility of the electric kiln and still exploit the rich and complex effects of smoke reduction. Two ceramists who use the electric kiln for their own experiments with reduction effects are Gerry Caplan and Dick Lehman (see pages 219 and 220).

MULTIPLE FIRINGS

Multifiring is a process in which pieces are fired more than once to obtain a desired visual effect. I have always felt that the term is quite different from *refiring,* which is the process of applying a glaze to cover a glaze that was not successful.

In the multifiring process, the ceramist fires to different temperatures during successive firings, starting at the highest temperature and then moving to lower temperatures. Ceramists often use this process to create complex imagery in unusual color combinations. No one part of the firing spectrum can produce all the colors available to ceramists. By multifiring, however, the ceramist can achieve the widest possible color spectrum.

The ceramist who employs the strategy of multifiring must be willing to spend a good deal of time and energy on each piece. The process requires great care, patience, and technical skill. Each successive firing puts stress on the piece and increases the likelihood of cracking. Contemporary multifiring is almost always carried out in an oxidation atmosphere in an electric kiln. Oxidation multifiring in the electric kiln stresses the clay body far less than the reduction fire of a fuel-burning kiln. Since the ware is already stressed from the multifiring process, it is best to avoid the stress or reduction firing.

GLAZING PROCEDURES: KEEPING NOTES

Carefully developed glazing procedures can be difficult to remember, especially if some time has passed since you last tried a particular procedure. I find it helpful to keep records of my glazing procedures in a notebook. I draw each piece before I glaze it (Figs. 7-14, 7-15), and then, in a step-by-step description, list the procedures I used while creating the imagery. I include an evaluation of each piece in the notebook after I fire the piece. Following are two examples of my note-taking procedures:

Cone 6 Carved Vase

1 Buff-colored body with carved imagery

2 Applied Mouse Black glaze to the interstices

3 Sprayed K15 Green base over the whole vase

4 Sprayed Corinth Blue at the top

5 Lightly sprayed Mouse Black at lip of the piece

Results: The glaze in the interstices heightens the carved imagery. The dark spray at the top of the piece softens the effect (Fig. 7-14).

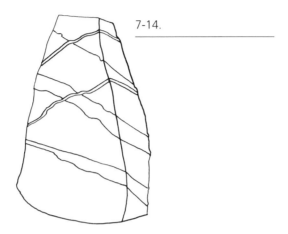

7-14.

Cone 3 Vase

1 Buff body

2 Poured Class Black glaze inside

3 Painted and sprayed terra sigillata over the outside of the piece

4 Poured Fairdale Cream over part of the surface

5 Poured Class Brown over part of the surface

6 Carved sgraffito imagery into the surface

Results: The two glazes contrast well with the terra sigillata. The sgraffito works best over the brown glaze (Fig. 7-15).

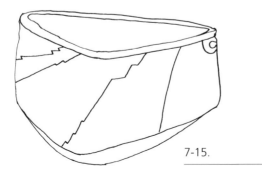

7-15.

TESTING IN IMAGE-CREATION PROCEDURE

Most ceramists are familiar with the glaze-testing process. However, image-creation testing is important as well (though it is less commonly carried out). Even small changes in image-creation methods can have a big impact on the look of the piece. Image-creation tests allow you to try a great variety of techniques quickly, without sacrificing finished pieces.

Here are some suggestions for successfully testing your image-creation procedure:

- Use a large test tile, about 12 × 14 cm.

- Use the same forming methods to create the test piece as you use in your work.

- Make sure you apply the surfaces and use the techniques in the order in which you intend to use them in your work.

- With other test tiles, try some variations of your intended image-creation strategy.

- Keep detailed notes of your procedures and include a description of the fired result.

- Label the tiles carefully.

IMAGERY IN CLAY

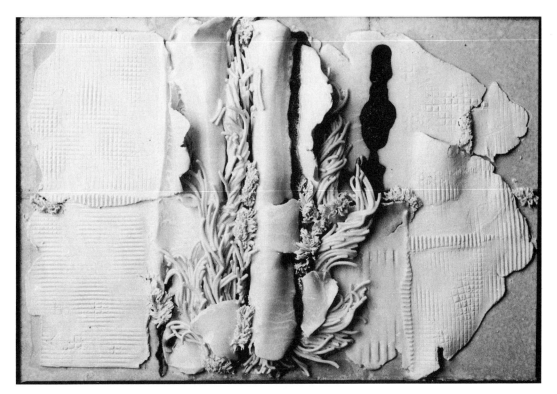

Ruska Valkova. Sofia, Bulgaria. Wall piece, 30 × 60 cm.

Valkova is interested in the character of her porcelain clay body. The forms she chooses reveal the character of the material when it is manipulated.

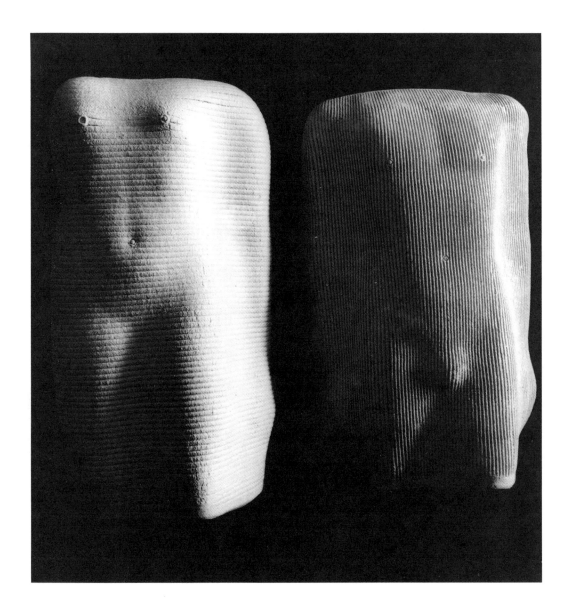

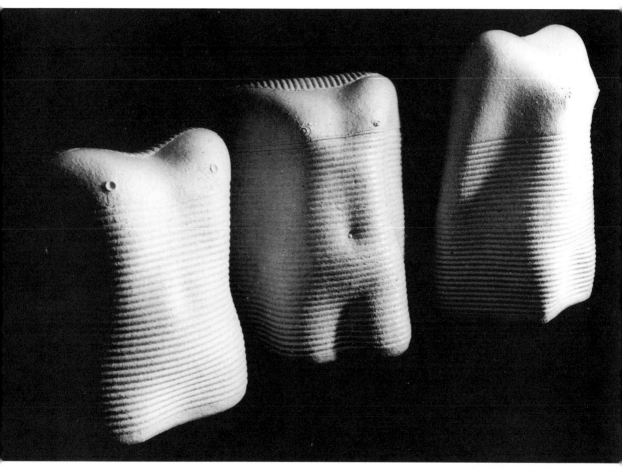

Vladimir Tsivin. St. Petersburg, Russia. "Figural Groups." Photos by Boris Smelov.

Tsivin uses grogged porcelain to create his figural pieces. The lively, warm character of the clay is an important aspect of the piece.

Angelo di Petta. Toronto, Canada.

This wall piece is an example of repetitive imagery in clay.

David Pendell. Salt Lake City, Utah. ''Spring, The Teapot's Dance Series,'' 27½ × 20 × 10 inches.

Pendell uses clay in a highly florid manner.

Richard Notkin. Myrtle Point, Oregon. OPPOSITE: ''Stacked Crates Teapot (Variation #6),'' Yixing Series, 7 × 5⅝ × 3 inches. ABOVE: ''Hexagonal Curbside Teapot (Variation #17),'' Yixing Series, 5 × 7⅞ × 4 inches. Courtesy of the Garth Clark Gallery, New York and Los Angeles. Photos by R. Notkin.

In making his pieces Notkin exploits the character of his stoneware clay bodies to create a complex storytelling imagery. Cone 5 to 6.

Ann Mortimer. New Market, Ontario, Canada. "Spring Tea," 6 × 14½ cm. Photo by Masao Abe.

In this work Mortimer uses clay in a highly sculptural way. Cone 04.

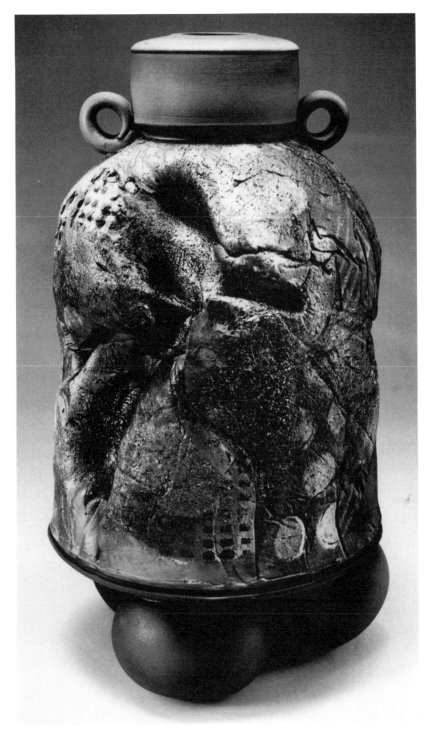

Sandra Blain. Knoxville, Tennessee. ''Canyon Markings,'' 19 × 10 × 10 inches. Photo by the artist.

Blain uses folded and ballooned clay imagery to create her forms. Cone 04.

CLAY INLAY AND COLORED PORCELAIN

Barbara Frey. Commerce, Texas. ''Round Trip Teapot #33,'' 6½ × 8½ × 4¼ inches. Photo by T. C. Eckersley.

Frey wedges body stains into a porcelain clay body. Cone 6.

Marylyn Dintenfass. New Rochelle, New York. "Paradigm Series: Checkers," 22 × 22 × 6 inches. Courtesy of the Everson Museum of Art, Syracuse, New York. Photo by Nick Saraco.

Dintenfass uses colored clays to create a painterly imagery. Cone 2.

158

Aurore Chabot. Tucson, Arizona. Two views of ''Black Brackish Bundle,'' 50 × 16 × 13 inches. Photos © 1992 Balfour Walker Photo. All rights reserved.

Chabot uses clay inlay and press mold techniques in her work. Cone 06/05.

Virginia Cartwright. Pasadena, California. ''Clay Inlay Teapot.'' Photo by Philip Starrett.

Cartwright uses a colored clay inlay technique to create her pieces. By using these clays rather than glazes as the finish for her pieces, she creates a rich surface. (She uses glazes in the interior of her pieces to help render them watertight.) Cone 3 to 5.

Curtis and Susan Benzle. Hilliard, Ohio. TOP: "On The Run," 4 × 5 inches. BELOW: "Morning Light," 3 × 4 inches. Photos by the artists.

The Benzles use a low-clay porcelain body with an inlaid colored clay technique.

GLAZE APPLICATION

Nancy Selvin. Berkeley, California. ''Teabowl,'' 3½ × 3 inches. Photo by Charles Frizzell.

Selvin used a heavily poured glaze to create a rich, fluid imagery. Cone 04.

Eileen Lewenstein. Brighton, England. "Triptych," 10 inches high.

An example of dip application of glazes. Lewenstein fires her work to 1250°C (cone 8 to 9).

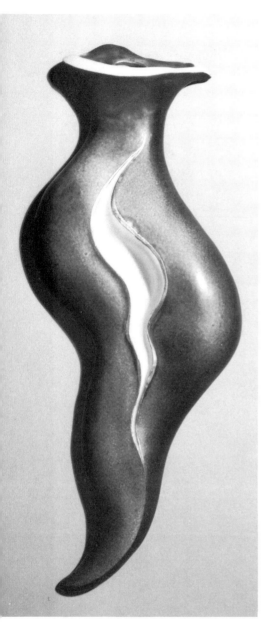

Robin Leventhal. Ann Arbor, Michigan. LEFT: ''Equipoise #1,'' 27 × 8 × 3 inches. RIGHT: ''Sculptural Form,'' 46 × 18 × 8 inches.

Leventhal's surfaces are sprayed using masking techniques. Cone 6.

Peter Lane. New Arleresford, England. TOP: "Bowl," 13 inches in diameter. BELOW: "Porcelain Bowl," 7¼ inches in diameter. Photos by the artist.

Lane uses an airbrush and masking techniques to enhance the surface of his porcelain pieces. Cone 8.

James L. Tanner. Janesville, Minnesota. "Dreamer," 22½ × 16½ × 3 inches. Photo by James Tanner.

In this wall piece Tanner has created most of the imagery using slip and trailing methods. He fires his work to cone 04 and cone 019.

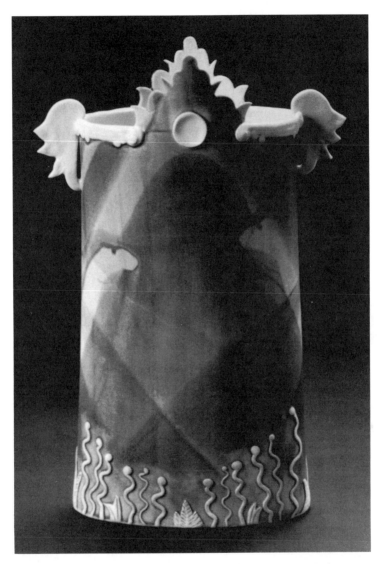

Henry Lyman. Spokane, Washington. "Amadeus Vase," 14 inches high. Photo by Rick Singer.

Note the extensive use of slip trailing at the base of the piece as part of the ornament. Cone 10.

PAINTED AND DRAWN IMAGERY

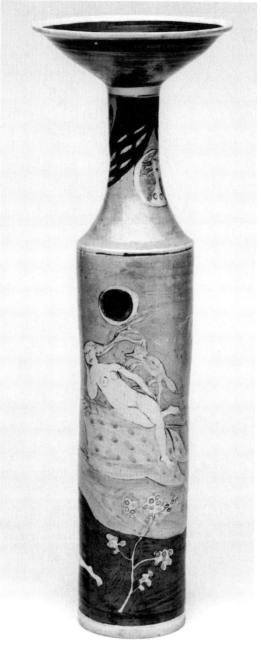

Eric James Mellon. Bognor Regis, England. Two views of "Tall Pot," 22 inches high. Photos by Chris Hadow Photography.

Mellon's forms act as carriers for his complex storytelling imagery. He fires his work to 1300°C (cone 10).

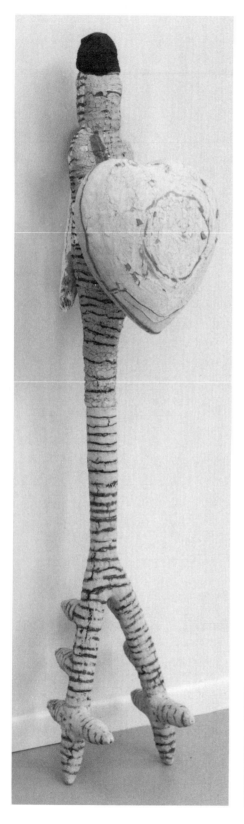

William Stewart. Hamlin, New York. LEFT: "Sower," 40 × 14 × 17 inches. BELOW: "Forked Heart," 60 × 13 × 15 inches.

These are strong examples of sculptural forms finished with drawn and painted imagery. Cone 04/03.

Richard Zakin. Oswego, New York. Wall piece, 37 × 24 cm. Photo by T. C. Eckersley.

Painted low-fire glazes and terra sigillatas with ceramic collage additions.

Jo Ann Schnabel. Cedar Falls, Iowa. "Sashay," 37 × 18 × 20 inches. Photo by
William Drescher.

*Schnabel paints the surfaces of her pieces so as to encourage a unity between
surface and form. Cone 3.*

Elyse Saperstein. Elkins Park, Pennsylvania. ''Tumi,'' 63 × 40 × 7 inches. Photo by John Carlano.

Saperstein uses terra sigillatas to create a rich painted imagery. Cone 03.

Roy Strassberg. Mankato, Minnesota. ''Stonehenge Jazz House #2,'' 36 × 25 × 4 inches.

Strassberg is working in a strong painterly vein in this piece. He fires to cone 04 for bisque and cone 06 for the final fire.

Deborah Black. Toronto, Canada. ''Wall Vase—View with Irises,'' 20 × 14½ × 2½ inches. Photo by Ed Gatner.

Black applies layers of colored slips and manipulates them with a scraper to create a painterly effect. She covers her pieces with a layer of clear glaze and fires to cone 04.

Andrea Johnson. Carmel, California. Bowl, 1 foot in diameter × 6½ inches deep. Courtesy of Winfield Gallery, Carmel, California. Photo by Lee Hocker.

Johnson creates strong painterly images using low-fire glazes. She fires to cone 06–05; most of her pieces are multifired.

Ina Orevskaya. St. Petersburg, Russia. "We'll Meet Again in Petersburg." OPPOSITE: "Art Is a Formidable Song Which Humanity Sings About Itself."

Orevskaya's painted work in porcelain is created with underglaze stains under a clear glaze. She first fires her work to 1400°C (cone 14) and then fires the imagery and final glaze to 800 to 850°C (cone 014 to 012).

Susanne Stephenson. Ann Arbor, Michigan. ''Dusk Water Rock,'' 3 × 27 × 27 inches. Photo by Suzanne Coles.

In this platter Stephenson has created semi-abstract imagery using brush and knife application of slips, glazes, and vitreous engobes. Cone 03.

John H. Stephenson. Ann Arbor, Michigan. "Helices Entwined," 14½ × 19½ × 15½ inches. Photo © 1989 Dick Schwarze.

Stephenson's complex, painted surfaces enhance the power of the form in his pieces. Cone 03.

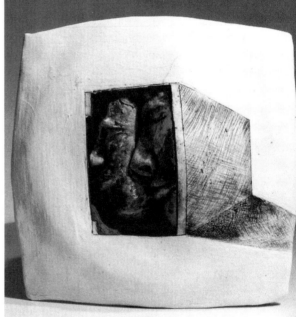

Denys James. Ganges, British Columbia, Canada. LEFT: "Cube Forward," 21.5 × 11 × 5 inches. ABOVE: "Merged and Contained," 13 × 15 × 4 inches. Photos by the artist.

James uses slips, colored grogs, stains, and oxide washes to create a complex, illusionistic imagery. He completes his pieces in a cone 04 single firing.

Nina Lyman. Spokane, Washington. "Cats Entwined Platter," 20 × 24 inches. Photo by Ric Singer.

Lyman uses low-fire glazes and sgraffito techniques to create her imagery. Cone 04.

Barbara Strassberg. Mankato, Minnesota. "Hermit Series: In Hiding #2," 17 × 5 inches.

Strassberg uses finishing underglazes to paint her pieces. Cone 06.

Donna Nicholas. Edinboro, Pennsylvania. ABOVE: ''Albion Diptych VII,'' 19 × 40 × 3 inches. OPPOSITE: ''Gyre VIII,'' 27 × 29 × 5 inches. Photos by Howard Goldsmith.

Nicholas has used painted imagery in these pieces to create strong imagery. Cone 04.

Mathias Ostermann. Montreal, Quebec, Canada. OPPOSITE: "Mermaid Teapot," 15 inches high. ABOVE: "Square Fish Bowl," 11 inches in diameter. Photos by Jan Thijs.

Ostermann's expressive power is derived from his command of the maiolica technique. Note the eloquence of the sgraffito line work. Cone 06.

William Brouillard. Cleveland, Ohio. "Majolica Platter," 26 inches in diameter.

In this piece Brouillard has used a low-fire, highly painted maiolica technique. The result is reminiscent of the Italian Renaissance masters of this medium. The first firing is at cone 05 and the second (a glaze fire) at cone 03.

Karen Thuesen Massaro. Santa Cruz, California. "Bowl #21," 3⅞ × 10⅝ inches. Photo by Lee Hocker.

In this piece Massaro uses glaze pencil, colorant washes, opaque and transparent glazes, and gold and silver lusters. Cone 10.

Karen Estelle Koblitz. Los Angeles, California. OPPOSITE TOP: "Della Robbia Still Life in the Garden of Eden," 23 × 41½ × 7 inches. OPPOSITE BOTTOM: "Japanese Still Life on Lily Box," 12½ × 14 × 8½ inches. LEFT: "Column #6—Italian," 27¼ × 11 × 11 inches. Photos by Susan Einstein.

Koblitz uses colored slips, underglazes, and glaze pencils under a clear glaze to create her highly painted pieces.

Karen Thuesen Massaro. Santa Cruz, California. "Dome Pins," approx. ⅝ × 2 inches. Photo by Lee Hocker.

In these pins Massaro uses opaque and transparent glazes and gold and silver lusters. Cone 05.

SGRAFFITO

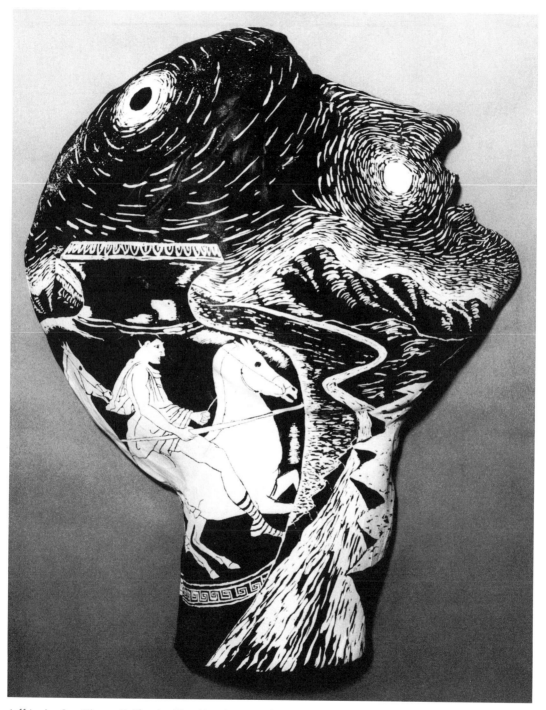

Jeff Irwin. San Diego, California. "Looking Up & Looking Back," 22 × 15 × 5 inches.

Irwin relies on the contrast between his dark underglaze and a very white clay body to create a strong image. Cone 03.

Giovanni Cimatti. Faenza, It-aly. LEFT: "Scoglio," 35 × 25 × 6 cm. OPPOSITE TOP: "Orma," 40 × 28 × 8 cm. OPPOSITE BOTTOM: "Campo," 33 × 40 × 1 cm.

Cimatti uses engobes and a sgraffito technique to create a unique imagery. He fires his work to 980 to 1000°C (cone 07 to 06).

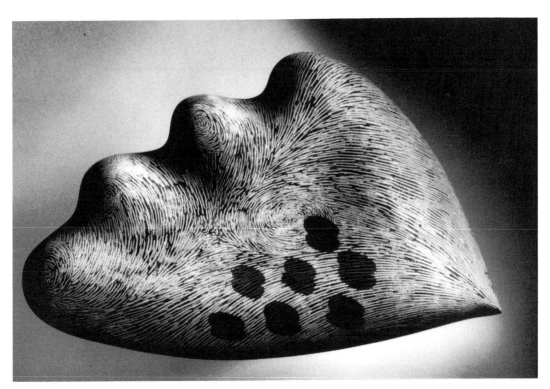

INTAGLIO IMAGERY AND MIXED MEDIA

Mary Barringer. Shelburne Falls, Massachusetts. Untitled, 6 × 9 × 15 inches. Photo by Wayne Fleming.

Barringer's austere intaglio surfaces emphasize her interest in clay and in the form. Cone 6.

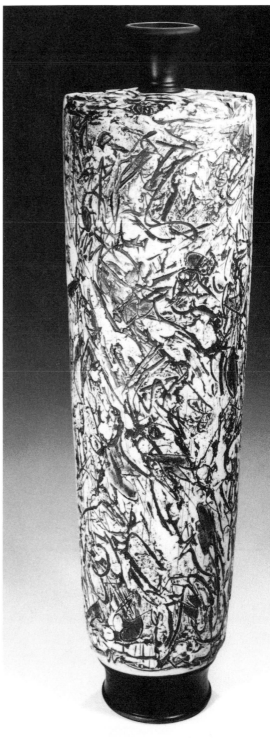

Regis Brodie. Saratoga Springs, New York. LEFT: ''Oval Form,'' 14 inches high. RIGHT: ''Tall Oval Form,'' 34 inches high.

Brodie has used a tighly woven intaglio imagery in these pieces. They are fired to cone 9/10. He then applies engobes, glazes, and lusters and fires again to cone 017 and cone 020.

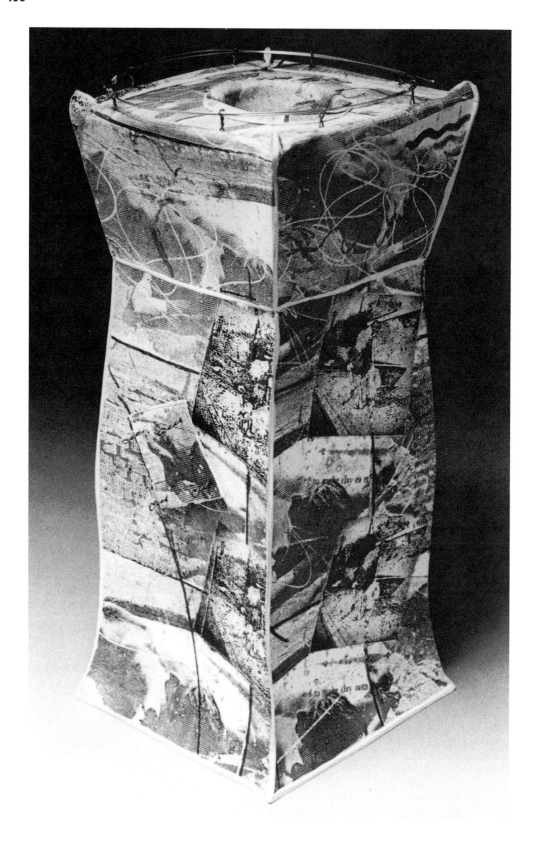

Les Lawrence. El Cajon, California. OPPOSITE: "New-Visions Vessel #36," 14 × 4 × 5 inches. ABOVE: "New-Visions Vessel #90A," 10 × 14 × 3 inches.

Lawrence uses a photo silkscreen technique to transfer a photographic image to the surface of his pieces. He manipulates the photographic imagery to transform it and take it beyond simple photographic reality. Cone 8/10.

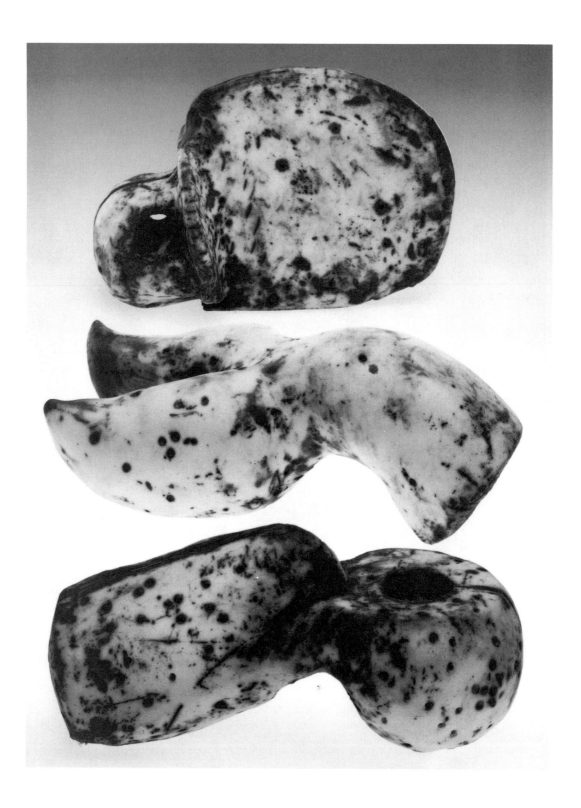

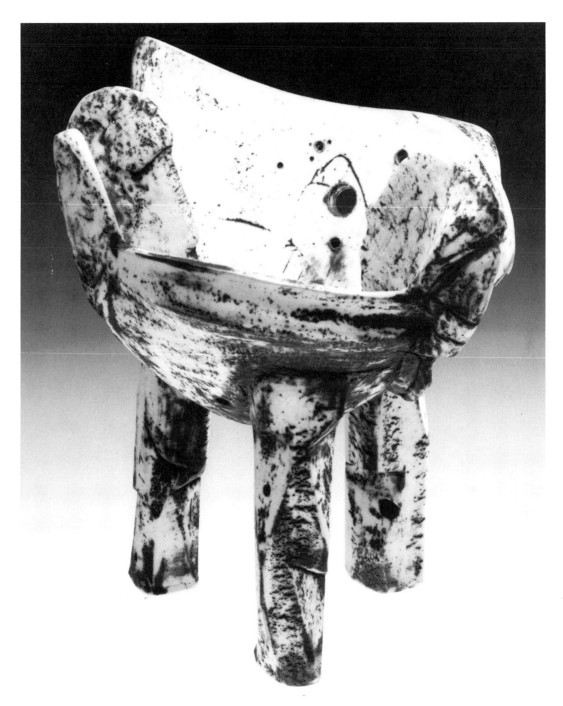

William Parry. Alfred Station, New York. OPPOSITE: "KFS—14," each approx. 10 inches long. ABOVE: "A Ringing in the Ears," 15 inches high. Photos by Brian Oglesbee.

These pieces feature a rich intaglio surface. Cone 6.

Katherine Ross. Chesterton, Indiana. "Thoughts on the Movement of Water," 4 × 3 × 7½ feet.

Ross uses ceramic elements with nonceramic materials to create her large sculptures. The ceramic elements are first fired to a cone 9 bisque and then glaze-fired to cone 6.

MULTIPLE APPLICATIONS AND MATERIALS

John Chalke. Calgary, Alberta, Canada. "Cracked Liberty," 3 inches high × 12 inches in diameter.

Chalke has developed a group of complex and demanding multifiring strategies which have resulted in a body of work that is highly idiomatic and audacious in character. Cone 6.

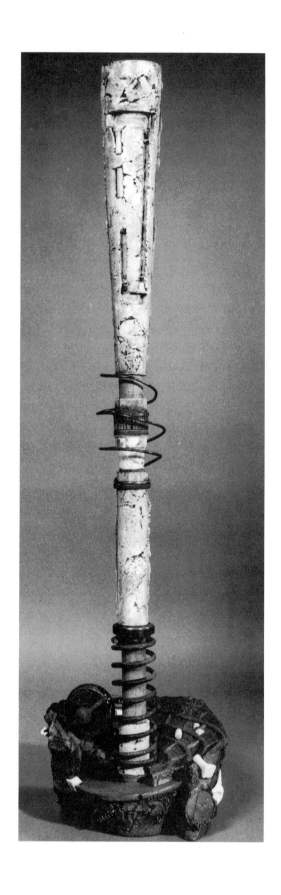

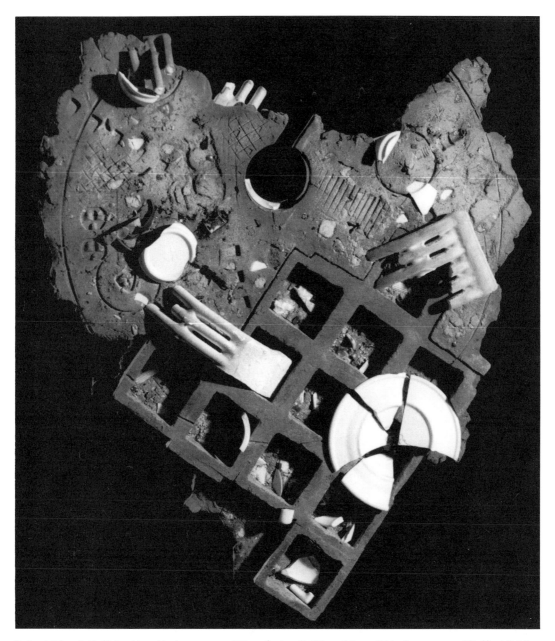

Robert Wood. Buffalo, New York. OPPOSITE: "Transfusion," 67 × 18 × 17 inches. ABOVE: "Baffled," 36 × 32 × 5 inches.

Wood uses terra sigillata, slips, stains, glazes, and various kiln parts to create these pieces. He fires his work in the low fire and mid-fire kiln.

Deborah Black. Toronto, Canada. "Fruitbowl with Bananas," 16 × 13½ × 4 inches. Photo by Ed Gatner.

Black creates an illusionistic space using layers of colored slips covered with a layer of clear glaze. Cone 04.

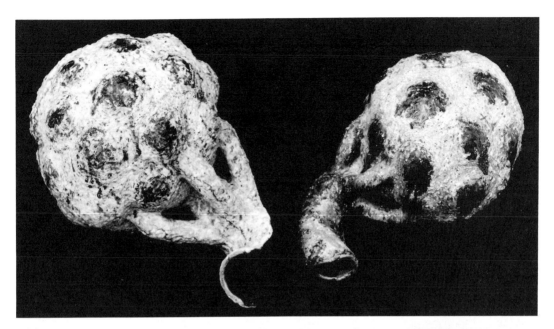

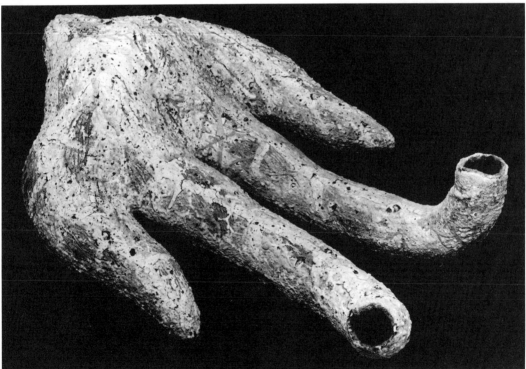

Zorin Kateranovski. Toronto, Ontario, Canada. TOP: "Ovaries," 14½ × 14½ × 22 and 11½ × 11½ × 18 inches. BELOW: "Seminal Vesicle," 11 × 24 × 37 inches. Photos by P. C. Brickell.

To create his restless surfaces Kateranovski applies layers of engobe, glaze, and glaze additives (such as glaze crystals, grog, casting slip, vermiculite, brass filings, stains, and coloring oxides). Cone 04 and 02.

Jamie Walker. Seattle, Washington. OPPOSITE: "Couple II," 52 × 28 × 25 inches. ABOVE: "Celestial Musings #9," 26 × 13 inches. Photos © 1991, 1992 by Eduardo Calderon.

Walker uses layers of different colored slips, glazes, and washes. The result is a variety of color and texture with an illusion of great depth.

Richard Zakin. Oswego, New York. Vase, 19 × 22 × 16 cm. Photo by T. C. Eckersley.

A red terra sigillata was applied before the bisque firing. After the bisque fire two glazes, a brown and a cream, were poured over sections of the piece. Then a sgraffito design was cut into the surface.

Angelo di Petta. Toronto, Ontario, Canada. TOP: ''Bowl.'' ABOVE: ''Painted Plate.''

Di Petta creates complex, multilayer, multisurface imagery using slips, stains, and glazes and a wide range of application strategies.

Georgette Zirbes. Ann Arbor, Michigan. OPPOSITE: ''Kostelec Conversations #3,'' 25 × 12 × 7 inches. ABOVE: ''Kecskemet Conversations #5,'' 24 × 14 × 11 inches. Photos by Suzanne Coles.

Zirbes uses a multilayered image creation strategy in which she applies slips and shards of prefired glaze to the surface of the wet clay. Once the pieces are bisque-fired, she applies a transparent glaze. Cone 6.

Barbara Strassberg. Mankato, Minnesota. ''Into Hibernation,'' 17 inches high.

Strassberg uses layering and overlapping of underglazes to finish her surfaces. She fires her work to cone 04 for bisque and cone 06 for the final fire.

Regis Brodie. Saratoga Springs, New York. "Orange Luster and Decal Bottle Form," 12 inches high.

Regis Brodie has used a multiple firing technique (both high-fire and low-fire) in this piece. The high-fire work is cone 9/10. Brodie then applies engobes, glazes, and lusters and fires again to cone 017 and cone 020.

Nancy Selvin. Berkeley, California. OPPOSITE: "Still-Life with Bottles," 3 × 2½ feet. ABOVE: "Teabowl," 3½ × 3 inches. Photos by Charles Frizzell.

Selvin has used a multiple firing technique to create this imagery. Cone 04.

Sandra Blain. Knoxville, Tennessee. OPPOSITE: "Hidden Hills Amphora," 16 × 10½ inches. ABOVE: "Solitude," 18½ × 14 inches. Photos by the artist.

Blain uses a complex strategy to create her imagery. While the slabs are still quite wet, she rolls burnable materials such as sawdust, loose fibers, and coffee grounds into the surface. She also rolls colorants into parts of the surface at this point and applies them again once the piece has been constructed and is leather-hard. A thin coating of clear glaze is applied to the bisque-fired piece to fix the colors and give them depth. Blain's work is bisque-fired to cone 04 and glaze-fired to a lower temperature.

John Chalke. Calgary, Alberta, Canada. "Dark Grey Cover with Grey Handle," 3½ × 11 × 17 inches.

An example of the unusual and highly personal ceramic surfaces Chalke has been able to develop using multifiring and multi-application strategies. Cone 6.

ALTERNATE FIRING TECHNIQUES

Dick Lehman. Goshen, Indiana. "Vase," 6 inches high.

Lehman uses a saggar-fired technique (in the electric kiln) for his smoke reduced ware.

Gerry Caplan. Pittsburgh, Pennsylvania. ABOVE: "Fragment," 10 × 12 inches. OPPOSITE: "Studio Floor Joint," 6 inches high.

These are smoke reduction pieces fired in the electric kiln. Gerry Caplan makes a good case for this technique in his work. The imagery is created with brushed and sprayed slips and glazes; stencils are used to mask parts of the surface. The work is first fired to cone 04 to 02. It is then fired to 700°C in a metal saggar stuffed with organic materials to create the smoke-reduction effects.

Nina Höle. Skaelskor, Denmark. LEFT: "Rolling Houses," 38 × 20 × 18 cm. OPPOSITE TOP: "Rolling Housewife," 28 × 53 × 28 cm. OPPOSITE BOTTOM: "Double Cross," 84 × 100 × 6 cm. Photos by Kristian Krogh.

Höle has created a fine example of strong sculptural imagery in clay.

THE ELECTRIC KILN

FIRING: BASIC CONCEPTS

Firing is the last hurdle the ceramist faces before the completion of the piece.

The Bisque Fire

Contemporary ceramists almost always fire their work twice. The first firing, the bisque firing, is essentially a preparation for the glaze application. A bisque piece provides a more stable ground for glazes, which are less likely to bubble and flake when applied to bisque-fired clay. Furthermore, bisque-fired pieces will not crack or break when immersed in glaze. Generally bisque kilns are fired to cone 08 or 06. In the second firing, the glaze is fired to maturity.

Controlling Heat Rise

Both bisque and glaze firing must be done carefully. To ensure the integrity of the ware and the glaze surfaces, the ceramist must fire in such a way that the heat rises gradually and steadily.

Firing the Bisque

To avoid cracking and shattering during the bisque firing, make sure that your ware is completely dry. Set the kiln on a low heat setting and leave the kiln door ajar for an hour or so at the beginning of the firing to allow residual moisture to escape.

The Glaze Fire

To avoid flaking and crawling during the glaze fire, make sure that the glazes are dry. Set the kiln on a low heat setting and leave the kiln door ajar for an hour or so at the beginning of the firing to give the glazes a chance to dry.

"Soaking" the Kiln

By making a few simple changes in the way you fire your electric kiln, you will see a vast improvement in the quality of your glazes. During the firing, the heat rise and loss must be controlled so that temperature changes occur gradually. This is especially important after the cone has bent. At this point many ceramists turn off the current and terminate the firing. However, if the current is kept on at a much lower level for an hour or so, the rate of cooling will not be as abrupt as it would be otherwise. This procedure, called "soaking," allows the kiln to lose heat slowly. As the kiln slowly cools, the glazes are given the time they need to develop visual textures (due to the development of microcrystalline formations on their surface).

LOADING THE ELECTRIC KILN

Kiln loading is complex and demanding and there are a number of pitfalls you will want to avoid. First, the piece must not be broken and the glaze surface must not be scuffed or smeared. Second, placing the ware is important: the ware must be placed at least one centimeter away from the coils to prevent it from shattering. Furthermore, you must be careful to prevent unwelcome bonds that often occur when glazed surfaces are allowed to touch each other or the kiln furniture during the firing. Finally, by placing your ware efficiently you will not waste any kiln space.

These are no easy tasks while reaching into an ill-lit and crowded firing chamber. Kiln loading is physically and mentally demanding, requiring great concentration and a good deal of expertise. It is important that you master this task well.

Kiln Furniture

The electric kiln is essentially an empty box. If the kiln is to be used efficiently to fire pieces of varying sizes, you will need "kiln furniture" for holding the ware. Kiln furniture is a flexible system of posts and shelves that can support ware of different sizes and volumes. The posts and shelves are made from refractory (nonmelting) materials that can withstand repeated heating and cooling.

Kiln shelves vary in size but are rarely more than 50 or 60 centimeters (20 or 25 inches) in length or width. In general, they are 1 to 1.5 centimeters (½ to ¾ of an inch) thick.

For electric kiln firings the shelves should be constructed of a substance high in the refractory material alumina. These shelves, which can be recognized by their light color (white or buff), are compatible with the oxidation atmosphere inside the kiln, can withstand heat shock well, and are economical.

Kiln posts range in height from 8 to 23 centimeters (3 to 9 inches) and are usually made from a refractory fire clay.

A modest yet important material for the kiln loader is kiln wadding. This mortar-like substance, made from grog and clay mixed with water, is placed between the post and the kiln shelf to prevent the shelf from wobbling (a common occurrence when using four posts).

The Loading Process

1 Measure the height of the ware to be fired. From this measurement you can determine what kiln posts you will need. If you need additional height, add fragments of broken kiln shelf on top of the posts. Start with fairly low pieces and reserve your tallest pieces for the top of the kiln.

2 Place the posts on the first shelf. For small shelves, use three posts; for large shelves (more than 1,200 square cm or 200 square inches), use four posts.

3 Load the ware on the first shelf. Exercise care, as a great many pieces are broken during the loading process. If you can see large empty spaces in the loaded kiln, you are wasting kiln space and electricity.

4 Place the second shelf on the kiln posts. If you are using four kiln posts for each shelf, check for wobbling by trying to move the corners of the shelf up and down. If the shelf wobbles, place kiln wadding under the wobbly post.

5 Place posts on the newly placed shelf and load this shelf with ware.

6 Continue until you have finished loading the kiln. If you are using cones to indicate conditions inside the kiln (a good idea even if you are firing with a kiln sitter [see page 231]), leave ample room for the cone on the shelf that is nearest to the spy hole. Look through the spy hole as you load the kiln to be sure you will be able to see the sides and tops of the cones clearly when you place them.

Making a Cone Pack

1 At least an hour or two before loading the kiln, make a cone pack by placing the cones in a wad of clay and grog. It should be approximately 10 cm long and 2 cm wide and high.

2 Use two cones, one that will bend one or two cones below the desired temperature, called the "guide cone," and one that will bend *at* the desired temperature, called the "firing cone." Gently insert the base of the cones into the clay. Set the cones at a slight angle to ensure that the first cone will not fall on the second.

3 Pierce the sides of the cone pack with a sharp tool to facilitate drying.

Cone Pack Placement

1 After the loading process is complete, the cone pack must be placed inside the kiln.

2 Place a flashlight in the kiln so that you can see the cones.

3 Check the height of the cone pack. If it is too low, raise it with a low post or pieces of broken kiln shelf.

4 Slide the cone pack into the kiln until you can see both cones clearly and will still be able to see them once they are bent.

5 Remove the flashlight and begin firing.

FIRING PROCEDURES

Bisque Firing

Bisque firings may be accomplished in one or two days (with an extra day for cooling). A one-day bisque firing is not quite as safe as the longer two-day firing, but if care is taken to ensure that the heat rise is slow during the early part of the firing, this is an acceptable procedure.

A Typical Day-Long Bisque Firing, Cone 08, 955°C, 1751°F

9:00 A.M.	Start the kiln on a setting that will produce a low heat rise. Leave the door ajar.
10:00 A.M.	Close the kiln door.
6:00 P.M.	The interior of the kiln is quite hot (around 600°C, 1112°F). Change the kiln setting to one that will produce a moderate heat rise.
7:00 P.M.	Turn the kiln setting to one that will produce a strong rise in heat.
8:00–10:00 P.M.	The kiln reaches maturation temperature. Turn off the kiln.

Second Day

11:00 A.M.	Open the kiln door a bit.
3:00 P.M.	Open the door completely.
6:00 P.M.	Unload the kiln.

A Day-Long Bisque Firing, Cone 08

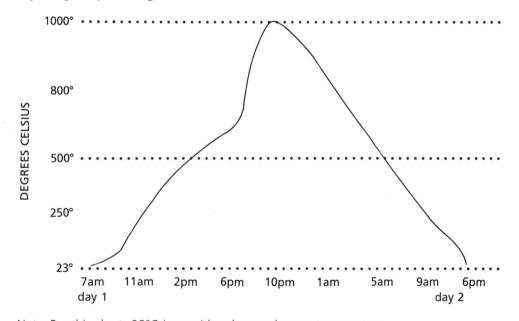

Note: For this chart, 23°C is considered normal room temperature.

A Typical Two-Day Bisque Firing, Cone 08, 955°C, 1751°F

This is the safest type of bisque firing for it ensures that the heat rise is slow during the early part of the firing.

First Day

3:00 P.M.	Start the kiln on a setting that will give a low heat rise. Leave the door ajar.
5:00 P.M.	Close the kiln door and allow the kiln to fire overnight.

Second Day

9:00 A.M.	The interior of the kiln is quite hot (around 600°C, 1112°F). Change the kiln setting to one that will produce a moderate rise in heat.
9:30 A.M.	Change the kiln setting to one that will produce a strong rise in heat.
11:00 A.M.–1:00 P.M.	When the kiln reaches maturation temperature, turn it off.

Third Day

9:00 A.M.	Open the kiln door slightly.
11:00 A.M.	Open the kiln door completely.
1:00 P.M.	Unload the kiln.

A Typical Two-Day Bisque Firing, Cone 08

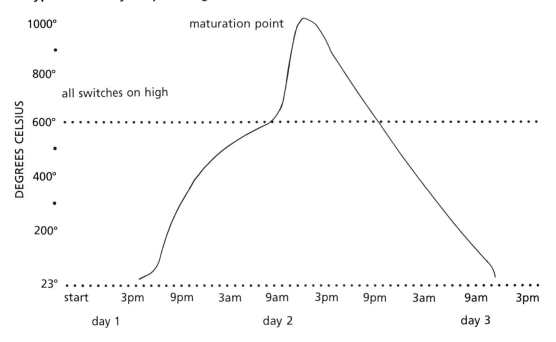

Note: For this chart, 23°C is considered normal room temperature.

Glaze Firing

Glaze firings may be accomplished in one or two days (with an extra day for cooling). While two-day glaze firings ensure good glaze results, glaze quality should not suffer in a one-day firing if a soaking procedure is followed.

A One-Day Glaze Firing, Cone 6, 1222°C, 2232°F

7:30 A.M.	Start the kiln on the lowest setting and leave the door ajar.
8:30 A.M.	Turn up the temperature setting to medium-low.
9:00 A.M.	Close the kiln door.
11:00 A.M.	The interior of the kiln begins to show color and its temperature approaches 540°C (1000°F).

12:30 P.M.	Turn up the temperature setting to medium or medium-high.
1:30 P.M.	The color has become fairly bright. The temperature is around 648°C (1200°F).
4:00 P.M.	The color is a bright orange. The temperature is around 1090°C (2000°F).
6:40 P.M.	The color is a light pink-orange as the kiln reaches maturation temperature. Turn the heat setting back to low and begin the soaking period.
7:40 P.M.	The color begins to return to its earlier bright orange and the temperature inside the kiln has fallen to 1040°C (1900°F). Turn off most of the switches and leave only one or two on.
9:00 P.M.	Turn off the kiln.

The Next Day

1:00 P.M.	Open the kiln door slightly.
4:00 P.M.	Open the kiln door completely.
6:00 P.M.	Unload the kiln.

A One-Day Glaze Firing, Cone 6

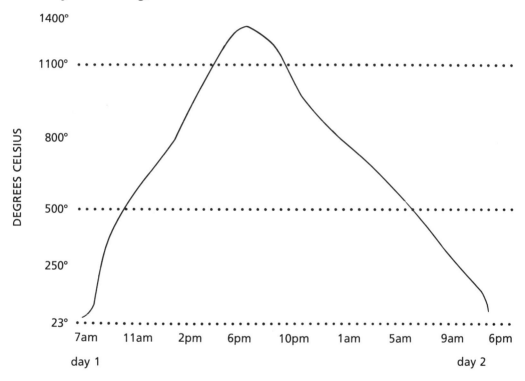

Note: For this chart, 23°C is considered normal room temperature.

A Two-Day Glaze Firing, Cone 6, 1222°C, 2232°F

The long preheat and soaking procedures made possible in a two-day firing encourage rich glaze surfaces.

First Day

3:00 P.M.	Start the kiln on the lowest possible setting and leave the door ajar.
4:00 P.M.	Turn up the temperature setting to medium-low.
5:00 P.M.	Close the kiln door and allow the kiln to fire overnight.

Second Day

9:00 A.M.	The interior of the kiln is quite hot (over 580°C, 1070°F). Turn up the temperature setting to medium or medium-high.
9:30 A.M.	Turn up the temperature setting to high.
2:00 P.M.	The color is a light pink-orange as the kiln reaches maturation temperature. Turn the heat setting back to low and begin the soaking period.
3:00 P.M.	The color begins to return to its earlier bright orange and the temperature inside the kiln has fallen to 1037°C (1900°F). Turn off some of the switches and leave only one or two on.
4:00 P.M.	Turn off the kiln.

Third Day

9:00 A.M.	Open the kiln door slightly.
12:00 P.M.	Open the kiln door completely.
2:00 P.M.	Unload the kiln.

A Two-Day Glaze Firing, Cone 6

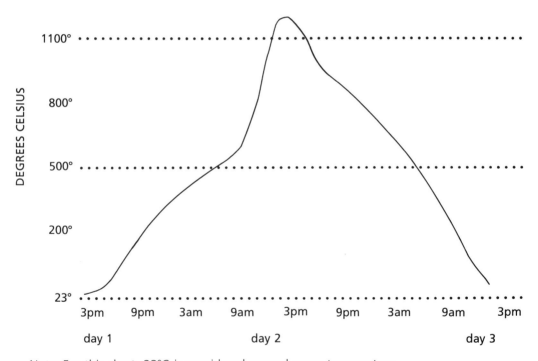

Note: For this chart, 23°C is considered normal room temperature.

COOLING THE KILN AND REMOVING THE WARE

Just as kiln loading and firing require patience and expertise, so does the process of cooling the kiln. It seems to be part of everyone's ceramic education to break a piece by taking it from the kiln while it is too hot.

While the temperature inside the firing chamber is above 700°C (1292°F), the kiln door should remain closed. Otherwise the ware will be subject to a rapid change in temperature and to heat shock. Once the temperature falls below 700°C (1292°F) mark, open the door slightly. As time passes you can open the door wider. Allow the kiln to cool at the rate of about 50° to 100°C (122° to 212°F) an hour. When the temperature reaches 500°C (932°F), open the door wider, but do not remove the ware from the kiln for about an hour. Only then can you safely unload the kiln.

Care in unloading is especially important when you are firing a new type of ware or when firing in a kiln you have not used before. Take particular care if you are using a new, highly insulated kiln. Such kilns retain heat efficiently and may have a slower cooling pattern than the kiln you are used to. It is best to wait until the ware is quite cool before unloading it.

PYROMETERS, KILN SITTERS, AND PROGRAMMED FIRING DEVICES

Pyrometers

Pyrometers are devices for measuring the high temperatures that occur in a kiln. They operate on the principle that voltage is created when two joined but dissimilar wires are subjected to high temperature. The voltage drives a gauge that indicates the *approximate* temperature inside the kiln. I emphasize the word "approximate" because pyrometers give only approximate readings. They are useful in that they indicate the rate of heat rise inside the kiln, but they are best used as supplements to pyrometric cones. Cones provide more accuracy and better guidance as to when to terminate the main part of the fire and begin the soaking process.

Limit Timers

Limit timers are clockwork devices that can be set to terminate the firing at a point an hour or so after the firing is normally over. They are safety devices designed to ensure against gross overfiring.

Kiln Sitters

Kiln sitters are devices that terminate the kiln firing automatically. They are very popular among ceramists as a labor-saving device. At one time I was opposed to such devices, but I no longer have such negative feelings about them, probably because I worked for a few months with kilns fitted with a kiln sitter. I found the kiln sitter to be accurate and reliable if I was careful in setting it.

Unfortunately, many ceramists who use a kiln sitter do not realize that it is a simple proposition to resume the firing after the kiln sitter has terminated the firing. This makes it easy to fire the kiln in a soaking mode for a time before shutting it off completely.

The Kiln Sitter Mechanism

In the typical kiln sitter design, a cone is placed inside the firing chamber and a current-control mechanism is placed in a box on the outside of the kiln. The cone is held by a retaining bar and a moving rod. When the cone bends, the rod falls. The rod activates the control mechanism, consisting of a push button and a hinged lever, mounted on the outside of the kiln. When the push button pops out and the hinged lever falls against the side of the box, all current to the coils is turned off.

Firing Down a Kiln Controlled by a Kiln Sitter

To be able to resume the firing, you will want to defeat the kiln sitter mechanism temporarily. To do this:

1 Lift the swinging lever back to its upright position and hold it in place.

2 Press the push button back to its open (inactivated) position; do this gently but firmly.

3 Gently and slowly let the lever down again without jarring.

4 Resume the firing (be sure, however, to set the switches on a low heat setting appropriate to the firing-down process).

5 Turn the heat setting to low.

6 After an hour or two, terminate the firing.

Note: Pyrometric bars, especially designed for the task, may be used in kiln sitters instead of a cone. Their untapered shape works well in the sitter mechanism and ensures consistant results.

Programmed Firing Devices

I have also had some experience using a kiln equipped with a programmed firing device. The programming required is an interesting but demanding process. Essentially this elaborate timing device requires the user to program the controller according to a firing schedule. I found that for firing a normal load the temperature control was good, but it was not accurate for firing an abnormal load. I felt that I still needed to use cones to make sure that I got the exact firing conditions I wanted. My co-workers found it easier to fire manually than to follow these procedures. This kiln did allow me to automate the firing-down process. Because firing down is important to me, I found this to be a great convenience.

Using a Programmed Firing Device as a Backup Device

It is also possible to use a cone sitter or any other automatic firing strategy can be used as a backup safety device. For example, if you are firing to cone 6, place a cone 8 in the mechanism; this will prevent gross overfiring. Meanwhile, use normal cones, placing them in front of the spy hole. When they fall, you will know that the kiln has reached the exact firing temperature you desire. Now you can manually terminate the firing or begin the soaking period. In this way you will have the advantage of safety associated with the kiln sitter and the advantage of flexibility associated with manual firing.

TECHNICAL ASPECTS OF THE ELECTRIC KILN

Electric kilns are simple structures, but they combine a complex group of technologies developed during this century. These include readily available electric current and sophisticated alloy, brick, and insulator technology.

The ceramist has to know a good deal about electric kilns in order to use them properly and keep them in good running condition. Good background knowledge also helps when purchasing a kiln. The next section deals with these "nuts and bolts" topics.

HOW THE ELECTRIC KILN WORKS

Kiln Elements

The kiln elements are the heart of the electric kiln. They are made from a special alloy formulated to withstand high temperatures. The elements are wound into tight coils placed inside the firing chamber in channels cut into its walls. Heat is produced by forcing a strong electric current through these tightly wound kiln elements. The result is friction, which causes heat. Since the firing chamber is a highly insulated closed box, the heat builds up steadily during the course of the fire.

Electric Service

The kiln elements are connected to a wiring harness and a group of switches located on the outside of the kiln. The switches control the kiln elements. A power cable connects the kiln wiring to a special heavy-duty electrical outlet. The current at the outlet is powerful (220 volts in North America, 240 volts in Great Britain). In most parts of the developed world electricity is widely available.

Insulating Bricks

The kiln walls are made from soft, porous, highly insulating bricks. Although bricks are, at least superficially, humble objects, the modern, highly efficient insulating brick is quite sophisticated and it plays a central role in electric kiln design. Electricity is an expensive source of heat, but in ceramics the expense is mostly offset by the efficiency of the closed-box design of the electric kiln. To be efficient, electric firing requires effective insulation. The porosity of the bricks makes them effective insulators.

After the firing is complete, the kiln is allowed to cool. Here again, the efficient insulating character of the insulating brick encourages slow cooling, which in turn encourages rich glaze surfaces.

Fortunately, insulating bricks make kiln construction easy because they are lightweight and simple to work with. A system of channels can be carved easily into the walls of the kiln to hold the kiln elements. The light weight of the bricks makes transportation from the factory somewhat easier—and less costly—as well.

ELECTRIC KILN CONSTRUCTION

Design

The two most common electric kiln designs available today are front loading and top loading. For many years most electric kilns were front loading, but recently top-loading designs have become more popular.

Top-Loading Kilns.   A top-loading kiln is a simple box or hexagon and each wall supports the other; together, the walls support the roof. The walls are bound together by a flexible metal shell, and the roof is hinged to the walls. The whole structure rests on the kiln floor, which in turn is elevated from the studio floor on metal legs. This is a simple and economical design.

Front-Loading Kilns.   Front-loading kilns are usually four-sided boxes with a door on one side. The wall holding up the door must be heavily braced. This design is difficult to build and expensive, but it does allow for quick and easy loading. Front-loading kilns are usually built to professional specifications. A well-designed, well-constructed front-loading kiln will last a long time.

The Kiln Roof

The roof of a top-loading kiln must be carefully designed because it will be subject to mechanical stress as well as heat stress. Well-made roof bracing will help prevent cracks, but even a well-braced roof will crack eventually under the stress of normal use.

The roof of a front-loading kiln is usually braced around its edges and undergoes little stress. Most are made with a shallow sprung arch, which is stronger than a flat roof.

Hinges

In the top-loading kiln design, the roof is hinged to the walls of the kiln. Heat escaping from the point where the roof and walls join can cause the hinge to deteriorate. Hinges are often designed with elongated arms to keep them away from the heat path.

The hinge structure of front-loading kilns has to support the weight of the door. Made from heavy-gauge steel, it is supported by the bracing elements attached to the outer kiln wall.

Segmented Kilns

Segmented kilns are made in sections and are easy to transport. This is especially true of large kilns, which are often segmented because it is easier to ship the kiln in segments than as a single heavy unit.

Some claim that segmented construction can give the ceramist some flexibility in firing. If you have a small load, you can unplug and remove one of the segments. This system will be convenient only if the segments are small and fairly light; awkward, heavy segments may be hard to unplug (and replug) and are hard to move without damaging the softbrick.

The most important design deficiency in many segmented kilns is the way electrical current is carried to the elements. Current may be carried by a plug and receptacle structure or by a series of cables. In the designs that have plug and receptacle connection, the manufacturer attaches a rectangular box structure that runs the length of each segment of kiln wall. These structures have a plug at one end and a receptacle at the other; the plug from one segment fits into a receptacle in the next segment. It is difficult to design a connection that can withstand the stress that naturally results when the heavy, awkward segments are assembled and disassembled. In response to criticism, some manufacturers have modified the design and allow the plugs and receptacles limited movement. This movement makes it easier to join the segments without breaking the fittings.

In designs that have a cable connection for the electric current, connections between one segment and another are made using an industrial-grade cable that plugs into a receptacle in the next segment. Kiln assembly is accomplished in one operation and current connection in another operation. This design is free of the physical stress that marks the plug and receptacle design.

Insulating Bricks

Electric kilns are made from lightweight, soft, insulating bricks that derive their insulating qualities from their porous character. They are usually made to withstand temperatures in excess of cone 8.

Wall Thickness

Top-loading kilns are usually constructed using bricks lying on their edges, while front-loading kilns are usually made with bricks lying on their sides. Edge placement creates a thinner wall than side placement. It is also lighter in weight and less expensive, but it is not as effective in containing the kiln heat as side placement. When bricks are placed on edge, a layer of insulation should be added between the bricks and the metal shell.

Insulation

When extra insulation is added in a top-loading or front-loading kiln, it is placed between the softbrick firing chamber and the kiln's metal shell. The insulation is usually made from spun kaolin fiber, paper, or block.

Element Channels

The kiln elements are set into a series of deeply carved channels set at an angle. The elements are fastened in the channels with refractory metal pins.

Kiln Elements

Kiln elements are made from an alloy that resists high temperatures, usually Kanthal A1, made by the Kanthal Company. The elements are connected to the wiring harness through small holes bored in the softbrick kiln wall.

Wiring Harness

The wiring harness holds the electrical wires that serve as the connection between the electrical outlet and the kiln elements.

Connecting Bolts

The connecting bolts directly connect the wires from the wiring harness to the kiln elements.

Switches

The switches control power to each element. The elements may be controlled by dial switches (also called infinity switches) or simple on/off switches. Either works well in a careful design.

The Metal Shell

Top-loading kilns are sheathed in a metal shell that binds the brick together. The shell can be fairly thin and flexible and often is given a high polish, which has neither a positive nor negative effect on performance. The underfloor and the kiln roof are usually braced.

The metal shell of front-loading kilns is usually made from rigid, heavy-gauge steel sheets. Stainless steel would be too expensive to use in the thickness required. The shell contributes a great deal to the structural integrity of the kiln. The corners and the door area are braced and welded. The door hardware ensures a tight closure during firing to contain the heat. Two door closures, instead of one, prevent the likelihood of the door opening accidentally.

Even Firing

Various strategies have been used to promote even firing in the electric kiln. Elements can be placed in the floor, walls, and door (in front-loading kilns) to ensure that the heat will be uniformly distributed.

Recently another solution has been found for this problem: bottom venting. Fan-driven bottom venting was originally designed as an efficient way to exhaust fumes coming from the kiln. Manufacturers found, however, that it also ensured a more even firing.

PURCHASING AN ELECTRIC KILN

Basic Choices

The information in this section will help you make an informed purchase of an electric kiln on the basis of its features. I have drawn up a series of questions that I hope will clarify your pattern of kiln use and help you decide on a particular design type and on a useful group of features.

Are you purchasing the kiln for a school or communal firing situation? Do you require great durability and a design in which safety considerations play an important role? If so, you should consider a front-loading kiln. Most ceramists purchase top-loading kilns because they are less expensive. Front-loading kilns, however, are appropriate for demanding environments.

If you decide on a top-loading kiln, you must choose between segmented and nonsegmented designs. Do you need the flexibility of a segmented kiln or the integrity of an unsegmented kiln? Many ceramists buy a segmented kiln and then never take advantage of the disassembly option (in many cases it is a difficult and tedious task to take the segments apart and reassemble them).

Segmented kilns do offer advantages in terms of flexibility. A segmented kiln that allows easy disassembly and assembly may allow you to work with unusually wide or tall pieces. Segmented kilns also offer an easy upgrade path: when you need a bigger kiln, you simply buy another segment. Finally, segmented kilns are easier to move.

What is your budget? If you are on a tight budget, a light-duty, top-loading kiln will be your best choice. If your budget is not so constrained, a heavy-duty, top- or front-loading kiln may be the best answer.

Construction Details

The Kiln Roof

When examining top-loading kilns, look for a roof that is well braced and easily replaceable. If you are considering a front-loading kiln, look for a well-constructed roof, preferably with sprung-arch construction, which is especially strong and longlasting.

Hinges

When examining top-loading kilns, look for an elongated hinge that is out of the heat path, heavy-gauge metal construction, and strong welds. If you are considering a front-loading kiln, look for well-constructed hinges made from heavy-gauge steel. Make sure the hinges are structurally sound.

Segmented Kilns

If the kiln has a plug and receptacle connection, look at the construction of the connectors that join the electrical system of one segment to the other. Make sure the plugs and receptacles are well made and set in mounts that have flexibility (so that they can be fitted together without breaking).

If the kiln has a cable connection, make sure the cable has enough slack to work well but is not so long as to get in the way. Also make sure that the cable is well insulated and firmly anchored.

Note: Even with design modifications that make the plug-connection system more reliable, there is a great likelihood that the connection will break if the segments are separated and then rejoined. In my opinion a cable connection is a much safer option and is a stronger and more trouble-free design than the plug and receptacle connection.

The Kiln Wall

Look for insulating bricks that will withstand temperatures in excess of cone 8. Also look for a brick thickness of at least 10 centimeters (4 inches) or brick backed by insulation. Look for insulation made from spun kaolin between the brick firing chamber and the shell. Also look for neat, deeply carved element channels.

The Kiln Elements

The kiln elements should be consistently wound to avoid hot spots and should sit snugly in the bottom of the channels, attached to the softbrick with refractory metal pins. The elements should be made from an alloy that resists high temperatures, such as Kanthal A1. They should be easily replaceable and fairly thick (thin elements burn out quickly).

Kiln Switches and the Wiring Harness

Look for smooth, positive switches. The wiring harness and connecting wires should be heat-resistant and of the highest quality. Look for easy access to the wiring harness so that element replacement is convenient. The connecting bolts must be well anchored. A loose connecting bolt will lower efficiency and encourage element burnout. Look for well-insulated wire (woven fiberglass insulation is best).

The Metal Shell

On examining top-loading kilns, look for good underfloor and roof bracing. On front-loading kilns, look for strong bracing everywhere, especially in the door area. Door hardware should be durable and well made and offer some flexibility in adjustment.

Even Firing

On top-loading kilns, look for floor-mounted elements or fan-driven bottom venting. Floor-mounted elements ensure that the bottom will be as hot as the middle and top of the kiln. Bottom venting (originally employed to vent fumes) is another method that ensures even firing.

On front-loading kilns, make sure that the kiln has been fitted with both floor- and door-mounted elements.

Guarantees

Many kilns come with limited guarantees. The kiln elements and the bricks cannot be guaranteed because they can fail for a great many reasons, some having nothing to do with their manufacture. For example, the ceramist may strike an element while placing a piece, or some glaze may fall on an element and break it. The switches and the wiring harness may or may not be guaranteed. The structure of the kiln should be guaranteed. While parts may fail in time, there is no excuse for premature failure. Look for the best guarantee you can find on the kiln structure. Perhaps your best guarantee of service is the reputation of the dealer.

USING AND MAINTAINING THE KILN

Using the Kiln

The following suggestions will help ensure the longevity of the kiln and kiln elements.

- Avoid striking the kiln elements while loading or unloading work. The elements become brittle as they age and break easily.

- Leave the kiln door ajar in the early part of the firing to vent moisture to prevent harming the elements and the kiln.

- If your kiln is top-loading, let its lid down gently and carefully. If you prop up the roof for cooling, use more than one prop and make sure that the props are of graduated height so that they all help support the lid.

Maintaining the Kiln

The following suggestions will help you keep the kiln working well.

- Test the kiln elements regularly with a small piece of Styrofoam. Turn on all the switches. Place the Styrofoam on each element in turn. If the element is working, the Styrofoam will melt slightly and indent. If this does not happen, the element is broken or disconnected.

- Clean the kiln regularly with a vacuum cleaner.

- Clean and reshape dented or crumbling bricks (softbricks are easily shaped with a simple kitchen knife).

KILN DIAGNOSTICS AND REPAIR

The electric kiln is a simple and reliable mechanism, but occasionally it may require repair.

Repair Sagging Elements

Never repair a sagging element when the element is cold and brittle. Turn the element on and let it get hot. Then, with two scrap pieces of wood, force the expanded, sagging elements closer together and up into their proper channel (Fig. 9-1). Patience and care are required for this operation.

Replacing Broken Elements

Even with careful use, kiln elements will eventually break. When they do, the elements will no longer transmit current and must be replaced. Though each brand of kiln has a different arrangement, replacing the elements is generally the same. The elements in their channel in the kiln wall go around the firing chamber once or twice. The ends of the elements go

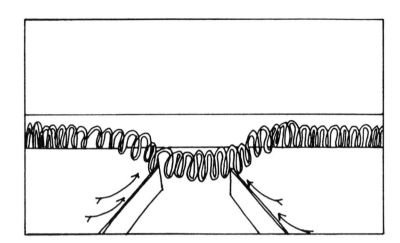

9-1. Push a sagging element into place with two pieces of wood.

through the walls to a wiring harness set in a control box placed on the outside of the kiln (see Fig. 9-2). Cut off all power to the kiln. After pulling the broken coil out of the channel and unhooking it from the wiring harness, place the new coil in the channel and connect the ends to the harness.

A Quick Temporary Weld

If you need to use the kiln while waiting for a new kiln element, you can temporarily weld the ends of the break together. With the power off, take a short length (4 cm) of broken element and, with a wooden tool, mesh this length of element with the broken kiln element. (Be sure the length of broken element is the *same* gauge as that of the element you are repairing.) Turn on the power to this element. You may have to repeat the process a few times, but the joining segment will temporarily weld itself to the broken element and carry the current. You will probably find this coil to be less powerful than the others.

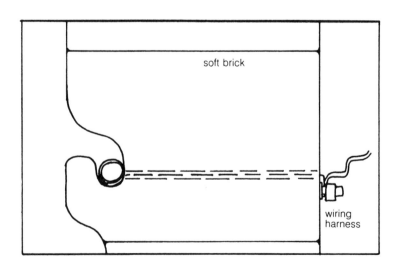

soft brick

wiring harness

9-2. Cross section showing element wiring.

Replacing Switches

Switches rarely break. When they do, however, they must be replaced.

On/off Switches. Replacements may be purchased from the kiln supplier or from your nearest electrical supply house.

Infinity Switches. Replacements must be purchased from the kiln supplier.

Cut off all power to the kiln. Remove the original switch from the control box (it is usually screwed to the front of the box with a threaded ring). Carefully unscrew or cut the leads from the connecting wires to the switch. Attach the leads from the connecting wires to the new switch. Mount the switch in the control box.

Structure and Brick Work

The Kiln Roof

It is very likely that after many firings the roof of a top-loading kiln will crack. When the roof must be replaced, it is best to buy a new one from the manufacturer. The roof of a front-loading kiln is subjected to far less stress and it will likely last for ten to twenty years. If the kiln is otherwise still in good shape, you can rebuild the roof if you are familiar with kiln-building techniques or know someone who is.

The Kiln Floor

The floor of the kiln rarely cracks, but it often must be replaced because glaze has dripped on it. You can avoid this by placing a kiln shelf on the floor of the kiln. Although this will cost you some loading space, it will not only protect the kiln floor but also will encourage a more even firing. Aside from this, many top-loading designs allow you to turn the floor over, thereby doubling the life of the kiln floor. When the floor must finally be replaced, buy a new one from the manufacturer or build a new floor using your own insulating brick and the old hardware. Insulating brick is surprisingly easy to shape and work.

Although small cracks may appear in the kiln wall, the cracks will rarely affect performance. Much more significant is damage to the bricks and the element channels during kiln loading or unloading. This problem is accentuated because the channels carved in the wall have exposed lips. These bricks may be reshaped or replaced.

If possible, reshape the bricks. Brick replacement can be a major job. Because the bricks in an electric kiln are not mortared together, they can be pulled out one by one. If, however, the brick to be replaced is halfway down the kiln wall, all the bricks above it must be removed as well. Furthermore, it is nearly impossible to remove bricks without removing the kiln elements attached to them. Then the elements will have to be replaced. Reserve this operation for a time when your kiln needs major repairs.

Wiring

Simple and obvious wiring problems can be handled by the ceramist, but it is important to know when to call on the services of an electrician. Sometimes a wire will come loose from its connection and merely need to be reconnected. It is reasonable for you to do this work. Save any major wiring chores for the electrician. Although their services are expensive, a knowledgable and sympathetic electrician will make sure that you can operate your kiln efficiently and safely.

CONNECTING THE KILN TO THE POWER SUPPLY

Installation

Electric kilns require a great deal of electrical current, and care should be taken during installation. They require special high-quality, high-capacity fuses, cables, and outlets. When it comes time to install an electric kiln, there is no substitute for the services of a qualified electrician.

Connections

Kilns of standard size (3 to 6 cubic feet) usually require 40 to 60 amps and 220 volts in the United States or 220–240 volts in Great Britain. These kilns are fitted with a heavy-duty power line and require two current-handling lines—a neutral line and a ground line.

Mixing current-handling lines with neutral or ground lines creates a fire hazard. Therefore a qualified electrician is the best person for this job. After examining the kiln wiring and testing the supply of electric current, the electrician will know how to connect the kiln correctly.

The Breaker Box

It is also necessary to install a breaker box in the circuit. This is an important safety device that is designed to prevent the interruption of current when it is needed for normal firing. If the kiln malfunctions, however, it will promptly interrupt the electric current. The electrician's job is to measure the normal amperage draw of the kiln and specify an amperage rating that would leave some leeway before the current supply would be interrupted. Only if the kiln malfunctions and requires more current than it needs in a normal firing will the breaker box interrupt the current supply.

Amperage Requirements

You may notice that your kiln's amperage requirements vary over time. This is because as kiln elements age, their resistance rises.

ELECTRIC POWER RATES

Rates for electric service can vary widely. Significant factors include geographical location, setting, and the time of the firing. Electric current is usually cheaper close to the source of generation; it is also cheaper in moderately built-up areas than in cities or in rural areas.

The setting can have a big influence on what you pay for electric service. If your kiln is located in your residence, most likely you will pay less than if it were in a storefront or factory setting. If it is in a factory setting, you may be asked to pay industrial rates. These rates are calculated according to complex formulas that reward large steady users and penalize small intermittent users.

Time of firing also may be a factor. In many areas rates may be cheaper late at night and on weekends. It pays to understand the rate structure and policies of the power company in your area before you make decisions about your kiln location.

SMALL ELECTRIC TEST KILNS

Most small test kilns are simple and inexpensive. They operate on normal household current (25 amps, 110 volts U.S.; 25 amps, 240 volts G.B.) and are quick-firing. The firing chambers are usually less than one square foot. They can be easily built or purchased. Because these kilns are portable and run on normal household current, they are more convenient than larger electric kilns, which require special wiring, outlets, and connections.

Test kilns are good for quickly testing glazes that you will later fire in a standard kiln. However, test kilns must be fitted with a heat controller in order to be used for this purpose. These tiny kilns cool very quickly, and it is rare that a quickly cooled glaze looks like a glaze from a standard firing. This is because quickly cooled glazes do not have a chance to develop the microcrystalline structure that marks (and enriches) the surface of glazes cooled in the normal way.

In a test kiln it is especially important that you control the heat buildup during the early part of the firing. Regular-size kilns have four or more coils and the heat can be controlled by simply turning on the coils one or two at a time, thereby enabling a slow and steady heat rise. Most small test kilns have room for only one coil, which is either turned off or running at top speed. To control the firing cycle and have the glaze mirror the look of glazes fired in a normal firing cycle, you will need a control mechanism to moderate the heat buildup. A simple and reliable controller can be installed that periodically interrupts the flow of current to the coil so that it runs only part of the time.

FIRING THE TEST KILN

The following firing cycle is recommended for test kiln firings:

1 Set the controller on very low current for ten minutes with the kiln lid open.

2 Close the lid.

3 After twenty minutes, turn up the controller to low.

4 Every twenty minutes, turn up the controller another notch—from low to medium low, then to medium high and high.

5 Leave the controller at the high setting until the cone bends and the kiln reaches the desired temperature.

Firing Down

1 Turn the controller down to medium.

2 After thirty minutes, switch the current from medium to low.

3 After another thirty minutes, switch the controller to very low.

4 Finally, after another thirty minutes, turn off the controller.

5 Allow the kiln to cool for an hour or two.

6 Open the roof bricks slightly.

7 After forty minutes, take off the lid.

8 After twenty minutes or so, empty the kiln.

You can fire finished pieces as well as test pieces in these tiny quick-firing kilns. Here again, controlling the heat is necessary because work that is fired too quickly may explode.

While you must tailor the form and size of the piece to the limitations of the kiln, in many cases this can be an interesting challenge. Small-scale ceramic objects such as jewelry are perfect for small test kilns. Since the kiln is portable and can be installed anywhere, it is ideal for ceramists on the move.

BUILDING YOUR OWN TEST KILN

There are many good test kilns on the market at reasonable prices. Some ceramists, however, choose to build their own. Test kilns can be built quickly and without specialized tools. The home-built kiln can be customized for the individual needs of the ceramist. The money saved varies from one-third to one-half the price of a purchased kiln. However, the best reason for building your own kiln is to gain knowledge of the process.

To construct the test kiln illustrated in this photographic series requires:

- Four K15 (or higher) soft bricks (place under the base and structure of the kiln)

- A board at least 25 × 40 × 1.5 centimeters thick to serve as a platform for the kiln

- Spun kaolin insulation to protect the board from heat

- Twenty-one K20 or K23 insulation bricks (you will cut one in half)

- Kanthal A1 coil wire (many kiln suppliers will be able to wind an element appropriate for this design)

- A current-interruption device (originally intended for use on kitchen ranges and often called a ''range controller'')

- Two industrial-weight electric cords and plugs (one each for the kiln and for the controller)

- An electric outlet box

- A box to hold the controller and the electric outlet box

Building the Test Kiln

1 Start with six insulation bricks. Place the bricks on a board to create the four walls of the kiln. Cut notches in the four corners, fitting the bricks tightly to create a stronger and better insulated structure (Fig. 10-1).

2 Cut two parallel grooves into the the insulation bricks that form the walls. The grooves should be one centimeter wide and deep (Fig. 10-2). Shape to support kiln element.

3 Place a board as a platform on which to build the kiln.

4 Place a layer of spun kaolin blanket over the board to protect it from the heat of the kiln.

5 Place a group of bricks (seven bricks and one more sawn in half) on top of this to serve as the kiln floor. Use a rasp to shape the bricks so that the floor of the firing chamber is raised slightly above the level of the kiln walls (Fig. 10-3).

6 Fit the kiln floor and wall structure together.

7 Bind the wall structure together with wire or banding, as shown in Fig. 10-4; banding is stronger.

8 At one end of the kiln, drill two holes for the connecting wires.

9 Stretch the kiln element and place it in the grooves cut in the wall. Anchor the element in place with refractory pins (Fig. 10-5).

10 Snake the connecting wires through the small drilled holes, connecting each wire to the harness. Connect a heavy-duty power cord and plug to these wires.

11 Place insulation bricks over the top of the kiln to form the kiln roof. And be sure to choose a location that is fireproof and well ventilated in which to place the kiln.

Note: You will see in Figure 10-6 that, after completion of the kiln, I added another layer of insulation brick under the kiln as a safety measure. I recommend that you place the extra layer of brick on top of the spun kaolin blanket and under the kiln floor as you see in the photograph.

Adding a Kiln Controller

In the setup illustrated, the current-interruptor is installed as an outboard device and placed alongside the test kiln (it is at the left in Figure 10-6). It can be plugged in when needed (during the heating-up and firing-down processes) and unplugged during the period when

10-1. Creating the wall of the kiln using insulation bricks. Note the notches cut in the corners of the kiln wall. Photo by T. C. Eckersley.

10-2. Forming the grooves that will support the kiln element. Photo by T. C. Eckersley.

10-3. Forming the kiln floor. Note the raised floor in the firing chamber. Photo by T. C. Eckersley.

10-4. The walls and floor of the kiln. The basic structure is nearly complete. Photo by T. C. Eckersley.

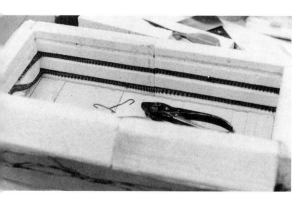

10-5. Place the kiln element in the element channels. Note the refractory pins used to anchor the element. Photo by T. C. Eckersley.

10-6. The completed kiln. Note the simple roof made from loose insulation bricks and the extra layer of kaolin blanket. Photo by T. C. Eckersley.

heat control is not necessary (during the height of the fire). This ensures a long life for the controller. Directions for building this device follow.

1 Build a small box.

2 Place mounting holes for the controller and outlet box as shown (Fig. 10-7).

3 Mount the range controller.

4 Mount the outlet box and face plate.

5 Connect the controller to the outlet box.

You may also wish to add a kiln controller to a 110-volt (240 volt in Great Britain) test kiln that you now own.

Firing with the Kiln Controller

Firing the test kiln with an outboard current controller differs from other firings in that the current interruption device can be plugged in when needed (during the heating up and firing down processes) and unplugged during the period when heat control is not necessary (during the height of the fire). This ensures a long life for the controller. To fire a kiln with an outboard controller follow the directions above for firing a test kiln, but in addition:

1 During the preheat and heat buildup part of the firing, plug the kiln into the controller.

2 Set the controller on the lowest setting for twenty minutes.

3 Turn the switch up every twenty minutes: switch the current from very low, to low, then to medium-low, then to high.

4 When the atmosphere inside the kiln begins to glow, quickly unplug the controller. Unplug the line from the kiln to the controller and plug the kiln directly into the electrical outlet in the wall.

10-7. Outboard kiln controller installation.

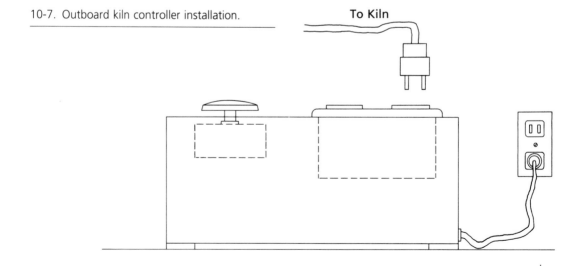

To Kiln

5 Continue the process until the cone bends and the kiln reaches the desired temperature.

6 To fire down the kiln quickly unplug the line from the kiln to the wall outlet and plug the kiln line into the controller. Plug the controller into the wall outlet. Turn down the switch on the controller every thirty minutes: switch the current from medium to low to very low.

7 At the end of this procedure, unplug both the controller and the kiln.

8 Allow the kiln to cool and unload it.

HISTORICAL HIGHLIGHTS IN OXIDATION FIRING

Since almost all of the work fired in the electric kiln is fired in an oxidation atmosphere, it is useful to know how ceramists worked with oxidation in the past. A great variety of work that deserves our attention has been fired in an oxidation atmosphere. We stand to gain much if we learn how this work was created.

Following is a chronological listing of the important styles, studios, and ceramists in the history of oxidation firing.

THE ANCIENT MIDDLE EAST (3000 B.C.)

In the Middle East ceramists have been firing in oxidation for millennia. Brilliant copper green glazes were developed in Egypt as early as 3000 B.C. In Iran during the Achaemenid period, (533–330 B.C.) potters created large, richly colored, lead-glazed wall reliefs that were fired in oxidation.

CHINA, TANG DYNASTY GLAZED WARE (A.D. 618–906)

Most Tang Dynasty ceramic pieces are low-fire, slip-decorated, and lead-glazed. These pieces were fired in oxidation in fuel-burning kilns. In fact, because lead boils and blisters in a reduction atmosphere, it was important for the Tang potters to fire in oxidation. They seem to have applied glazes composed entirely of lead over their clay bodies and colored slips. Lead glazes of this sort bond with the silica and alumina in clay and need contain no clay. However, because they contained no alumina, these glazes ran and flowed in the fire. The Tang potters compensated for this strong glaze flow by leaving the lower part of the piece unglazed. The imagery was patterned, abstract, and very colorful.

THE MIDDLE EAST (7th to 12th Centuries)

The period from the seventh to the twelfth century in Iran was marked by great interest in glaze technology and mastery of image creation techniques. Potters painted their vessels and tiles in elegant, inventive, and colorful ways. They used many slip and glaze techniques, the most common being the application of a clear alkaline or lead glaze over painted slips. They fired their pieces in low-fire oxidation.

CHINA, SUNG DYNASTY, T'ZU CHOU WARE (A.D. 960–1279)

T'zu Chou ware is an oxidation-fired, highly decorated, mid-fire stoneware made in North China. The style was developed during the Sung Dynasty. The imagery has a graphic orientation that relies on the use of a slip or glaze that does not blur or run in the fire. In some pieces, slips were partially carved away to reveal the contrasting color of the clay body; the piece was then covered with a clear glaze. In others a dark glaze, most probably based on a high-impurity clay, was applied over a lighter body and partially carved away (for more on the T'zu Chou image creation strategies see *Ceramics: Mastering the Craft*).

JAPAN, MOMOYAMA PERIOD, ORIBE WARE (1568–1614)

Oribe ware was intended for use in the tea ceremony. The buff or oyster-colored clay body, the brilliant color, and the crisp graphic imagery all clearly speak of a high-fire oxidation or neutral atmosphere. The Oribe potters used a complex image creation strategy: a single piece might be ornamented with two colors of clay, a black glaze (used to create linear imagery), slips, and a translucent green glaze.

CHINA, EARLY CH'ING DYNASTY PORCELAINS (1644–1780s)

During the early part of the Ch'ing dynasty potters attained great proficiency in the use of complex multifiring techniques. Based on porcelain forms, their pieces were fired initially in a high-fire reduction kiln, with subsequent firings in oxidation. In these lower firings the potters used the then-new palette of brilliant, low-fire overglaze colors, which originated in France.

11-1. Japan, Oribe ware bowl, nineteenth century, 2⅝ × 7¼ inches. The Everson Museum, Syracuse, New York, P.C. 81.44.1, gift of Mr. and Mrs. V. Cole. Photo © Courtney Frisse.

In this piece two surfaces were used. In the first, covering the middle of the piece, dark slips were painted on a white slip ground and covered with a thin, clear glaze. The second surface is a translucent, dark green glaze poured over unslipped areas.

11-2. Turkey, Isnik, sixteenth or seventeenth century. The Everson Museum of Art, Syracuse, New York, P.C. 90.246. Photo © Courtney Frisse.

The potters of Isnik formed this piece using a white body; they then applied slips and finally a thin, clear glaze. This work is low-fire, but its inspiration was the high-fire porcelain of the Ming and Ch'ing dynasties in China.

Ch'ing dynasty porcelains (the very best of which were created for the Imperial House) are aristocratic, fastidious, technically imposing, and highly inventive.

TURKEY, ISNIK WARE (15th–19th Centuries)

Isnik ware is a product of the Ottomans from the city of Isnik in the western part of Turkey. It is a white slipped ware painted with blue, green, black, purple, and red; these are covered with a transparent, shiny glaze. The color is rich and brilliant; especially noteworthy is a tomato red derived from a very pure high-iron clay. The imagery is florid and carefully painted.

GERMANY, DRESDEN PORCELAIN (Early 18th Century)

By the seventeenth and eighteenth centuries in Europe, porcelain from East Asia was highly prized and much sought after by those wealthy enough to afford it. The methods used in making and firing porcelain were well known in their country of origin, China, as well as in the rest of east Asia. The European ceramists, however, did not know how to make porcelain until the early eighteenth century, when Johann Friedrich Böttger, an itinerant alchemist, and Ehrenfried Walther von Tschirnhausen, an experimenter and theoretician, developed a European version. European porcelain differed somewhat from that of Asia: the European materials dictated the use of a complex recipe, and tradition dictated the use of the oxidation fire.

As in the Chinese porcelains of the Ch'ing Dynasty, there is a strong emphasis in this work on brilliantly colored, low-fire overglazes. The pieces are inventive, highly refined, and sophisticated.

ENGLAND, JOSIAH WEDGWOOD (1730–1795)

Josiah Wedgwood was a potter, ceramic experimenter, and entrepreneur. Early in his career Wedgwood worked with dark vitreous clay bodies fluxed with dark, high-iron clays. These dark bodies were limited in color. For his ''Jasper body,'' Wedgwood introduced barium, a colorless flux that allowed him to create a rich, stony surfaced, light-colored clay body. This body lent itself to a broad range of colorants. Wedgwood's first experiments with barium-containing bodies resulted in a straw-colored body; then in 1774–1775 he produced a white-colored Jasper ware. Later he developed a group of bodies colored with stains: blue of three shades, lilac, pale pink, grayish-green, olive green, yellow, and black, all fired in an oxidation atmosphere.

FRANCE, BARBOTINE WARE (Late 19th Century)

Barbotine ware, developed in the 1870s, featured slip-painted decoration covered with a clear glaze. The painting style was usually highly pictorial, imitative of oil painting. This work was low-fire and lead-glazed.

U.S.A., AMERICAN ART POTTERY (Late 19th–Early 20th Century)

The American Art Pottery movement began in 1876 when Mary Louise McLaughlin, a china painter from Cincinnati, Ohio, saw Barbotine ware from France at the Centennial Exposition in Philadelphia. She decided to work in this manner and developed a method in which she used painted slips under a transparent, shiny lead glaze.

This new work attracted attention and encouraged others to enter the field. The imagery of American Art Pottery was derived from a painted slip decoration, covered with a clear lead glaze. From the beginning most American Art Pottery was fired in oxidation. Most of this work was made in the form of the decorative vessel. When we talk of the American Art Pottery movement we talk of the work both of individuals working in their studios and of factories with tens or even hundreds of workers each responsible for a small part of the work.

The Rookwood Pottery (1879–1950s)

In 1879, Maria Longworth became interested in the work of her fellow Cincinnatian Mary Louise McLaughlin and took up a slip painted style. The Rookwood Pottery, which she founded, quickly became the most pretigious of the American Art potteries. By the mid-1880s the staff grew and training improved. In 1884 the spray atomizer was introduced; it was used to apply slips that served as a background for the painted imagery and helped create unusually rich effects. In 1904, in response to interest in mat glazes, Rookwood devel-

11-3. Newcomb Pottery. "Lily Vase," 1902, Esther Huger Eliot, decorator. The Everson Museum of Art, Syracuse, New York, P.C. 89.9.1. Photo © Courtney Frisse.

Colored slips were painted over a light-colored ground. A transparent lead glaze was then applied to finish the piece.

oped the "vellum glaze." This was both semi-mat and translucent (almost to the point of transparency); it was applied over colored slips just as the clear glaze had been. Thus the Cincinnati Faience style was kept alive, albeit in a modified form.

The Newcomb Pottery (1895–1940s)

The Newcomb Pottery was founded in 1895 as part of Newcomb College in New Orleans. The studio was founded to encourage and train young women for entrance into the field of ceramic decoration. In their early work the potters at Newcomb adopted the Cincinnati slip painting techniques, but combined them with a sgraffito line engraved in the surface of the clay. The result was a complex interplay between soft painted slip images and a crisp, engraved line. By 1911 the Newcomb potters were moving away from the Cincinnati technique with its shiny glazes. In their new work they applied a translucent mat glaze over the slips. The effect is softer and richer than that of the earlier technique, and the overall character is markedly different, though only the glaze was changed.

George Ohr (1857–1918)

George Ohr's work is expressive of a strong and independent personality. He threw and decorated in an unusually direct and energetic style. His brilliantly colored slip images are virtuosic examples of the decorator's art: they are deftly applied, expressive, and fanciful. He applied his slips with sponges and brushes. He covered them with a rich, clear lead glaze and fired in an oxidation atmosphere.

William H. Grueby (1867–1925)

In the early 1890s Grueby founded a tile studio. In 1897 he began producing mat-glazed art pottery, for which there seemed to be a ready market. The Grueby glaze, characterized by a soft, velvety, nonreflecting surface, was fired in an oxidation atmosphere. It is opaque and monochromatic, its color most often a strong ocher/green, though a golden ocher was also used. Although Grueby's glazes remain unanalyzed at this time, we can assume that they are lead glazes, high in clay and in opacifying materials such as tin or zirconium. Grueby's mat glazes proved extremely popular and influenced many contemporary art pottery firms to switch at this time to lead-fluxed mat glazes.

Fredrik Hurten Rhead (1880–1942)

Rhead was born in England to a family long associated with the potteries. After a thorough training, he came to the United States in 1902. He was active as a ceramist in the early and mid-twentieth century. Rhead, an intense and volatile man, worked for many of the most important art potteries, moving from job to job. His work in studios and factories is marked by an astonishing variety of image creation strategies. These include painted slips, slip trailing, glazes of all sorts—shiny, mat, and even dry surfaced—resist and sgraffito techniques, and mold-formed work whose polychrome imagery derives from the use of two colors of casting slip. The variety and intellectual power of his work with image creation techniques is noteworthy.

The Roseville Pottery Company (1890–1954)

The Roseville Pottery Company in Zanesville, Ohio, never had the prestige of such establishments as Rookwood but much of the work from this factory was well made and carefully designed. Early work at Roseville employed the Cincinnati faience techniques and individually hand-painted images.

The Overbeck Studio (1910–1937)

This pottery was operated in Cambridge City, Indiana, by three sisters: Hannah Overbeck (1870–1931), Elizabeth Gray Overbeck (1875–1937), and Mary Frances Overbeck (1878–1955). Hannah designed and occasionally decorated pieces as well; Mary did decoration, finishing, and glazing; and Elizabeth formulated and made clay bodies and glazes and did wheel forming and firing. The best work of the Overbeck studio is marked by a reserved and highly stylized ornamental imagery. The pieces were fired in a low-fire oxidation atmosphere in an updraft, fuel-burning kiln. The surface was created by using a colored slip covered with a satin-surfaced, transparent glaze. Only now is their work getting the attention it deserves.

Van Briggle Pottery (1901–The Present)

The Van Briggle studio was founded by Artus Van Briggle in 1901 in Colorado Springs. After his death in 1904, his wife, Anne Van Briggle continued production. The clay body is buff-colored and of moderate absorption; the glaze is a soft, rich mat. The glaze is almost always marked with a strong crackle pattern. The most common colors are a copper blue and a chrome-tin crimson. This glaze probably derives its character from barium.

FRANCE, TAXILE DOAT (1851–1939)

In 1887 Doat began work at the Sèvres factory outside of Paris. He became well known for his work in porcelain and stoneware. At the turn of the century Doat was commissioned by an office of the French government to write a technical and aesthetic overview of ceramics in France. This book, *Grand Feu Céramique,* was to influence the course of ceramics in both the old and the new worlds. Doat worked primarily in oxidation-fired porcelain. Perhaps his most interesting work featured the demanding and rich-surfaced glaze type known as flowing mat. These unusual glazes are highly fluxed and low in alumina and silica. The low melting power of the fluxes resulted in a mat surface. The low alumina percentages encouraged strong glaze flow.

U.S.A., ADELAIDE ALSOP ROBINEAU (1865–1929)

Robineau was born in Middletown, Connecticut, in 1865. She learned the craft of china painting in her late adolescence and after a time began to teach it. When she and Samuel Robineau were married in 1899, they founded the magazine *Keramic Studio*. By 1903 she turned from china painting to creative studio work in porcelain. In that year she obtained the book *Grande Feu Céramique* by Taxile Doat, which strongly influenced the course of her work. She fired at cone 9, in an oxidation firing, fuel-burning kiln. Almost all of her work was ornamented with excised and carved imagery and then finished with rich glazes. She used a wide variety of high-fire surface finishes and glazes, including crystal glazes (both mat and shiny), flowing mat glazes, nonflowing mat glazes (she called them fixed mats), and finally a black or umber metallic stain.

U.S.A., ART POTTERY (1910–1920)

Teco Pottery (ca. 1904–1909)

This pottery in Terra Cotta, Illinois, was owned by William Day Gates. While he had the pieces made in a factory context, Gates aimed to create work that was quite inexpensive and, at the same time, of the highest quality. Only one glaze base, a low-fire recipe fluxed with lead, seems to have been used throughout the course of the Teco production. This glaze base has an unusually high amount of tin, which gives it a silvery character, great opacity, and a satin surface. This surface was emphasized by a simple, monochromatic sprayed application. Generally this glaze base was colored with copper, which produced a cool green.

Fulper Pottery (1910–1925)

The Fulper studio was incorporated in 1899 as the Fulper Pottery Company in Flemington, New Jersey. They introduced their Art Pottery line, Vasekraft, in 1909. Fulper pieces were

11-4. Adelaide Alsop Robineau. "Monogram Vase," 1905, 12⅜ inches high. The Everson Museum of Art, Syracuse, New York, P.C. 16.4.17. Photo © Courtney Frisse.

Robineau worked with porcelain bodies and applied highly flowing, low-clay glazes. Here she used a flowing mat glaze. The dark, irregular patches at the bottom of the piece are the result of two glazes flowing together in the fire. Low-clay glazes of this sort can produce crystals, which you can see at the neck of the piece.

11-5. Adelaide Alsop Robineau. "Viking Vase," detail, 1905. The Everson Museum of Art, Syracuse, New York, P.C. 16.4.1. Photo by Lorenz/Main Street.

Robineau used the rich flow patterns of her glaze to complement her simplified and stylized carved forms. Here the glazes flow and interact around and over the carved imagery. In some places the glazes follow the carved forms; in others they flow in a less controlled manner. The total effect is richer, more complex, and less literal than it would be if stiffer and less active glazes had been applied.

cast-formed, using a tan-colored stoneware clay. Their highly flowing glazes (both shiny and mat) were splashed and poured over the piece to create an imagery that relied on the rich patterns that can be created by exploiting glaze flow.

Rookwood Soft Porcelain

In 1915 the Rookwood potters introduced their "soft porcelain." These were mold-formed pieces made from a mid-fire porcelain with bas relief imagery (created in the mold) and finished with satin mat oxidation-fired glazes. This marked a break for Rookwood from the low-fire, lead-glazed Cincinnati Faience methods of the past.

The Cowan Pottery (1919–1931)

In 1919 the ceramist R. Guy Cowan established a studio whose work was characterized by highly stylized Art Deco variations on traditional themes. Much of the work was mold-formed. The Cowan decorators employed a group of rich glaze surfaces and a wide variety of glaze application techniques including dipping, pouring, and painting.

THE 1930S IN THE UNITED STATES

Ceramics, like all other art movements, suffered during the 1930s, and few were able to build careers during this period. Two ceramic artists who did were Henry Varnum Poore and Victor Schrekengost. The large establishments suffered as well; but while most closed, the Roseville factory continued to flourish during this period.

Henry Varnum Poore (1887–1970)

Poore was a painter and self-taught ceramist who worked during the 1930s and 1940s. His ceramic work was finished with painted slips and lead glazes fired in an oxidation kiln. Poore was trained as a painter and draftsman rather than a potter and approached pottery from this standpoint. His work features strong concentration on imagery. However, because Poore was very sensitive to the ceramic medium, he was able to exploit the possibilities of the medium in an effective and individual way.

Viktor Schreckengost (1906–   )

A ceramist and industrial designer, Schreckengost worked with great effectiveness in both the vessel form and ceramic sculpture during the 1930s. He is well known for a series of slip-painted bowls covered with a clear glaze and a series of complex figurative earthenware sculptures.

Roseville Pottery

As we have seen the work of the Roseville Pottery was originally part of the American Art Pottery movement. However, shortly after 1908 all individual decoration of artware was

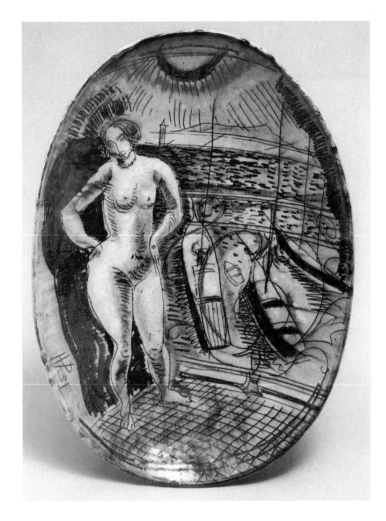

11-6. Henry Varnum Poor. "Platter with Nude," 1931. The Everson Museum of Art, Syracuse, New York, P.C. 40-348. Photo © Courtney Frisse.

Poor was trained as a painter. The lucid, freely done imagery shows a confident drawing style as well as a real sensitivity to the ceramic medium.

abandoned. Designs were either embossed or applied by decalcomania, and decoration was executed en masse by unskilled labor. Through the difficult times of the thirties this strategy proved very effective. Roseville flourished while other studios went out of business. This work, a highly designed "Art Moderne" style, featured low-fire shiny lead or lead/boron glazes.

ENGLAND (1940s and 1950s)

Lucy Rie (1902–   )

Lucy Rie was born in Vienna and trained there by Michael Powolny, a ceramist and teacher. She left Austria for England in 1938 and established a studio in London. Her work is characterized by simple thrown porcelain forms and high-fire, soft-surfaced oxidation glazes. These surfaces are often enriched either with a sgraffito line, the bubbled texture of dry surfaced glazes applied one over another, or a brushed application of a manganese stain.

11-7. Roseville Pottery.
Wincraft, "Circle Vase," 1948.
Photo by Thomas C. Eckersley.

In this piece colored slips are covered by a transparent glaze. Slip surfaces of this sort are easy to control, but they are often flat and unrelieved by any visual texture. In this piece a white spatter provides relief from the flat quality, creating an interesting "faux granite look."

Hans Coper (1920–1981)

Coper was born in Germany but went to England in 1939. Because of the war his life was unsettled for a number of years; in 1943, after discharge from the army, he made England his home. In 1946 he met Lucy Rie and began to work as a potter. His forms, strongly vessel-oriented, are thrown and altered. The highly designed and intellectual character of these forms is offset by his combed, rough surfaces, finished with stains and fired to cone 9 in an oxidation kiln.

U.S.A., MARY AND EDWIN SCHEIER (1940s and 1950s)

In the 1940s and 1950s, unlike most of their contemporaries, Mary and Edwin Scheier produced a body of work mostly fired in oxidation. Some of their most notable pieces were marked by complex sgraffito imagery. At this time there was great interest in the art of peoples of nonwestern culture: this is mirrored in the Scheiers' imagery with its depictions of stylized figures with "cowrie shell" eyes and lips and direct frontal gaze.

THE RISE OF INTEREST IN OXIDATION FIRING (1950s to The Present)

By the 1950s in the United States there was great interest in high-fire reduction stoneware, and for a time oxidation firing was in eclipse. Little work was done in the area and it was commonly felt that results from the electric kiln had to be pallid and lacking in vitality.

11-8. Mary and Edwin Scheier. 1957–1958. The Everson Museum of Art, Syracuse, New York, P.C. 60.13. Photo © Courtney Frisse.

The Scheiers were known for their linear imagery. In this example sgraffito imagery was engraved into the surface of the high-clay, nonrunning glaze.

By the 1960s, however, the pendulum had swung once again. In the 1960s and 1970s the movement called Funk or Pop Pottery originated on the West Coast of the United States. It was characterized by the use of imagery derived from popular culture and by the use of low-temperature glazes fired in the electric kiln.

Although ceramists no longer work in the Funk idiom, its influence remains strong and most ceramists work in the oxidation fire. At first this new interest in oxidation was limited to the low fire, but by the 1970s mid- and high-fire oxidation had adherents as well. At present the majority of ceramists in North America use the electric kiln, which is popular in England too. It is now very difficult, due to environmental laws, to fire with a fuel-burning kiln in the built-up areas of England (especially around London). There is a great deal of interest in mid- and high-temperature oxidation firing and a great deal of interest in image creation methods that work effectively in oxidation.

GLOSSARY

Alumina: One of the basic building blocks of clays and glazes. Clays, feldspars and frits contain alumina. Alumina is refractory (nonmelting); and promotes plasticity and strength in clay bodies and durability and viscosity in glazes. Glazes with a moderate alumina content tend to be mat, opaque, nonrunning, and very durable. Glazes with a high alumina content may be dry-surfaced.

Ball clay: A fine-particled plastic clay used in clay bodies to improve workability and plasticity. Ball clay encourages shrinkage and cracking, so its use must be carefully controlled; do not use in amounts over 50% in low fire bodies or 15% in stoneware bodies.

Bisque firing: A preliminary firing of unglazed ware. While bisque firing temperatures may vary widely, the most common are cones 08–06. The bisque fire prepares the work for glaze application; the ware can be immersed in the watery glaze without cracking or breaking down.

Calcining: The process of heating a material in order to drive off organic impurities, water or carbon (these are driven off as gases). Calcined materials are added to recipes to make them more stable. For example, in high-clay glazes the plasticity of the clay may cause difficulties during firing; the process of calcining will help diminish the plasticity.

Clay body: A compound of clay and nonclay materials chosen for their individual characteristics that, when combined, meet the specific requirements of the ceramist.

Colloids: Materials with a very fine particle size. Colloidal particles are useful to the ceramist because they encourage workability in clay bodies and good suspension in engobes and glazes.

Colorant: A mineral or compound of minerals used to color ceramic materials. The most common colorants are: iron oxide, cobalt oxide or carbonate, copper carbonate, rutile (a compound of titanium and iron), and manganese dioxide.

Crawling: A glaze defect in which the glaze forms in separate droplets during firing rather than forming a smooth, durable surface. When crawling occurs on a dust- or dirt-free bisque-fired piece, it generally indicates that the glaze formula is too viscous because of an overly high clay content.

Deflocculant: An alkaline material that encourages clay particles to repel each other.

Deflocculated: The result of adding a deflocculant to clay. Clay bodies that have been somewhat deflocculated (because of alkaline melters in the formula) lose much of their plasticity. Clay that has been highly deflocculated becomes completely nonplastic and far more liquid. Deflocculated clays are used in slip-casting to make clay bodies liquid.

Engobe: Originally this term was related to the concept of an envelope—that is, an overall coating of slip. Slips used as engobes were almost always porcelain slips intended to disguise modest clay bodies so that they would look like porcelain. The term has come to mean a porcelain or semiporcelain slip applied in any fashion. Engobes have a clay content of 25 to 50 percent and a nonclay content of 50 to 75 percent.

Filler: A neutral material. Clay body fillers are nonplastic and are added to recipes to increase strength and lower shrinkage. Their particle size varies from very coarse to very fine. Fillers added to slips, engobes, and glazes are finely ground, nonmelting, nonclay materials that strengthen and stabilize the recipe.

Fire clay: A coarse, large-particled clay that contributes strength and workability. In itself it is only moderately plastic, but it may significantly enhance plasticity by encouraging particle-size differentiation. Fire clays tend to be buff, tan, or ocher in color as a result of their moderate iron (1 to 3 percent) and titanium (1 to 3 percent) content.

Flocculant: An acidic material that encourages the aggregation of clay particles. (For its opposite, see *Deflocculant,* above.)

Flocculate: To cause clay-particle aggregation (which can encourage plasticity) by adding acidic materials.

Flocculated: A state in which clay particles tend to aggregate or clump together. The clay mass acts as a coherent, workable material that can be shaped and formed.

Flux: An oxide that causes melting, including the oxides of barium, calcium, boron, sodium, potassium, and silicon.

Frit: Manufactured compounds containing silica, alumina, and melters. While more expensive than many materials used in ceramics, they are highly valued and used widely for their stabilizing and strong melting powers. Sodium, calcium, and boron are the most common melting ingredients in frits.

Glaze: A glassy coating especially formulated to fit over a clay form. Glazes contain silica, alumina, and melters.

Greenware: Finished ware that requires drying before it can be fired.

Grog: A coarse-particled filler for clay bodies. Adding grog to a clay body ensures that the body will contain a wide variety of particle sizes. Grog also impedes warping and encourages durability.

Ground silica (also called flint): A finely ground silica powder, free of impurities, which is an important source of silica in ceramic recipes (clay bodies, slips, engobes, and glazes).

Inlay: A process in which clays of more than one color are worked together to create a multicolored clay piece.

Kaolin: Clay distinguished by its great purity and whiteness. Kaolins tend to be less workable than other clays, but their beauty and refined character compensate for their lack of workability.

Maiolica: A brilliantly colored glaze-painting technique employing an opaque white glaze that serves as a ground for the application of glaze color. This technique was used extensively in European ceramics in the fifteenth and sixteenth centuries.

Maiolica glaze: A low-fire glaze made mainly of lead oxide (a strong melter) and tin oxide (an opacifier). These opaque white glazes are formulated to work well with applied color.

Maturity: When applied to clay bodies, "maturity" refers to an optimum point at which warping and brittleness are kept to a minimum and the absorption rate is reasonably low. When applied to glazes "maturity" refers to the point at which the glaze produces a desired effect. Generally glazes are called mature when they are fully melted in the fire and are glassy in surface.

Melter: A compound that causes melting, facilitating glaze formation. Melters include silicates, feldspars, and fluxes.

Opacifier: A material that blocks the passage of light through the glaze, thereby rendering the glaze opaque. Opacifiers encourage the formation of small bubbles or crystals that change the structure of the glaze and block the passage of light.

Opax: The trade name of a comparatively pure and powerful zirconium opacifier.

Oxidation: The combination of a material with oxygen.

Oxidation firing: A firing in which there is ready access of oxygen to the firing chamber at all times. Electric kilns in general are constructed in such a way as to fire in oxidation.

Plasticizing agent: An ingredient added to a clay body recipe to improve workability. Two types of plasticizer are available: organic plasticizers and fine-particled clay plasticizers. Organic plasticizers such as yogurt or beer encourage bacterial action, which makes the clay elastic and ''slippery.'' Fine-particled materials such as bentonite and colloids increase the variety of particle sizes in the body and lessen the impact of coarse particles.

Porcelain: A pure white clay body that is translucent where thin. Porcelain bodies contain no more than half white clay; the other half is composed of ground silica (flint) and feldspar. Because of their low clay content and nonplastic character, porcelains are difficult to work with; however, their beauty compensates for their limited workability.

Pyrometric cones: These narrow pyramids mimic clay bodies and glazes and react to the combination of time and temperature (often called ''heat work''). As time passes and the temperature increases, the cones soften and bend. The ceramist uses the deformation of the cone as an indication that the clay bodies are mature and that the glazes are melted and glassified and firing complete.

Reduction firing: Firing with a minimum amount of oxygen. In reduction firing, the potter interrupts the flow of oxygen to the firing chamber of the kiln at certain crucial periods during the firing. This is most naturally accomplished in the fuel-burning kiln. Reduction firing strongly influences the character of clay bodies and glazes.

Refractory: Resistant to heat.

Rutile: A colorant compound of iron and titanium.

Shivering: Glaze patches forced away from the ware, leaving sections of unglazed body visible, especially at the corners and edges of the piece. Shivering occurs when the glaze shrinks less than the clay body. It can be eliminated by increasing the shrinkage of the glaze or by decreasing the shrinkage of the clay body.

Silica: A crystalline material that, along with alumina, is one of the building blocks of all clays and glazes. The sources of silica are powdered silica, feldspars, clays, talc, and wollastonite. Silica promotes plasticity and durability in clay bodies and glaze flow, durability, and a glassy melt in glaze formulas.

Slip: A mixture of clay and water. The word is used in two ways: (1) as a viscous mixture of clay and water used to hold clay pieces together and (2) as a mixture of clay (or clays) and water, with perhaps some nonclay materials, that is applied to the surface of the clay piece for decorative effect.

Soft paste porcelain: Traditionally, porcelain is fired to high temperatures, 1260°C or higher (cones 9–12). Porcelain fired to lower temperatures must contain strong melters (due to the refractory character of the clay content of porcelain); these strong melters, unfortunately, deprive porcelain of some of the dense and durable qualities for which it is so admired. However, the material is still quite durable and beautiful. These slightly softer, less dense, highly fluxed clay bodies are termed soft paste porcelain to distinguish them from porcelain itself, which is fired to a higher temperature.

Stains: Calcined compounds of kaolin and naturally occurring ceramic colorants that have been modified by additions of oxides, which affect their color. Stains offer a whole new color palette for the ceramist. The colors are brilliant, safe, and reliable. Stains are added to the glaze in varying amounts, usually 3 to 8 percent of the total recipe. While relatively expensive, they have certain advantages over naturally occurring colorants: they are predictable and reliable and their color is WYSIWYG (what you see is what you get). Because they may be adversely affected by an ingredient in the recipe, they must be tested before normal use.

Stoneware clay: A term used in the United States to designate a raw clay that matures at cones 8–9, is buff or tan color in oxidation, and is plastic and workable. The color is due to a moderate iron content (1 to 3 percent) and titanium content (1 to 3 percent). Stoneware clays are valued for their blend of workability and strength.

Stoneware clay body: A body that contains a high percentage of clay and a low percentage of nonclay materials (some stoneware bodies contain no nonclay materials). The clays used often contain some iron and titanium impurities (2–4 percent iron, 1–2 percent titanium). In color, stoneware bodies are buff, tan, orange, or brown. They have good particle-size variation and are workable and durable. They mature at cones 6–11.

Talc body: A clay body that contains a significant amount of talc (usually 25 to 50 percent). Talc is a strong melter and is especially useful in low- and mid-fire clay bodies. Because of the slippery character of the talc, these clay bodies are fairly workable even though they are low in clay.

Terra-cotta red clay: A high-iron clay. Because of its impurities, especially iron, this clay is valued for its rich, hearty color. The iron content often exceeds 6 percent. Iron serves not only as a coloring agent but as a powerful melting flux as well. These clays, therefore, are often used as an ingredient to encourage clay body maturity. Terra-cottas mature at a low temperature; they are usually fired in oxidation to take advantage of their rich earth-red fired color.

White body: A clay body containing only white and colorless clay and nonclay materials. Porcelain bodies are high-fire and translucent bodies; other white bodies may be opaque or intended for the lower fire.

White stoneware: An opaque white clay body. These bodies, like porcelain, must contain only white or colorless materials such as kaolins, ball clays, and non-iron-bearing melters. Unlike porcelain, they may have a fairly high clay-to-nonclay ratio, and they tend to be much more workable than porcelain.

Whiting (calcium carbonate): A common melter used in slips, engobes, and glazes and occasionally in clay bodies. In both clays and glazes it promotes durability; in glazes it also may promote rich surfaces.

Wysiwyg: "What you see is what you get." In ceramic parlance this means: "If it goes into the kiln with a particular look, it will come from the fire with a similar look." Originally imported from the computer world, the term has a useful place in our lexicon.

Zirconium opacifiers: A group of similar compounds, all containing the element zirconium, which interferes with the passage of light in glazes. Not all zirconium opacifiers are of equal purity or opacifying power. However, all tend to produce similar results, and substitutions between various zirconium opacifiers are often successful. In general, additions of 10 to 12 percent are sufficient to ensure opacity.

APPENDIX A: MATERIALS AVAILABILITY

Because ceramic materials are bulky and expensive to ship, you will find many available only locally. Unless you live in the northeastern part of North America (as I do), you may not have access to some materials that I can find easily. In this situation you will have to substitute materials that are similar to those I call for in my recipes. (I have to make the same kind of substitutions when using recipes developed in Great Britain.) I have found over the years that one or two of the various substitute materials I have tried will probably work well. However, I cannot emphasize too much how necessary it is to perform tests on any recipes you modify before you commit yourself to their use.

I did not always believe that materials substitution was such a useful strategy. In the first edition of this book I listed materials by trade name; in this edition I do not, as this does not encourage substitutions. Because I hope to encourage ceramists to experiment with all sorts of substitutions, I now list glaze materials using generic labels. For example, where I previously called for *Old Mine #4 Ball Clay*, I now use the generic term *ball clay*. At the end of this appendix, I list the trade names for the materials I use in my recipes.

FOR CERAMISTS WORKING OUTSIDE NORTH AMERICA

Most of the materials called for in my recipes will be available to you (especially as I list them generically). However, two materials that I use a great deal, Gerstley borate and Barnard slip clay, are not always available outside of North America. If you wish to try my recipes and these materials are not available, you will need to find appropriate substitutes for them.

Gerstley borate is a non-water-soluble source of sodium and boron. If Gerstley borate is not available, you can substitute boron-containing frits. Because these frits contain a great deal of silica, substituting frit for Gerstley borate may substantially change the look of the glaze. Often the frits will cause greater melting and shinier surfaces. I suggest that you experiment with a number of boron frits available to you; you may find that one is more appropriate than the others. If you are technically knowledgeable, you may wish to analyze the recipe and redo it using locally available materials.

I use Barnard clay, a dark-colored clay, in clay bodies and glazes. Dark, high-impurity clays of this type are fairly common and you may find that you have a local equivalent. Basalt, a high-impurity volcanic rock used in clay bodies and glazes, has some similarities to Barnard clay and you may wish to try this when I call for Barnard.

The terra-cotta clay available to you may have a different character from the terra-cotta clay I use in my clay bodies and glazes. The terra-cotta clay I use, Cedar Heights Redart, is unusually high in silica. Yours may be lower in silica and may react differently in the fire. I suggest that you experiment with the terra-cotta clays that are available to you in order to find a good substitute.

The clays I call "stoneware clays" may also seem to be unavailable to ceramists outside of North America. However, this is a labeling problem, not a matter of availability. Outside North America (in English-speaking countries), clays that I would call stoneware are usually termed "plastic fireclays." When I refer to a stoneware clay, I refer to a raw clay that matures at about cone 8 or 9 (1263°–1280°C), is buff- or tan-colored in the oxidation fire, and is quite plastic (due to its high varied particle sizes, including a good percentage of fine particles). This clay is well suited for use in stoneware bodies, but it also works well in mid- and low-fire bodies.

SUGGESTIONS FOR CERAMISTS WORKING IN ENGLAND AND CANADA

England

Etruria Marl may be used whenever I call for red clay. Basalt may be used where I call for Barnard clay. The clays I call "stoneware clays" are usually called "fireclays" or "plastic fireclays" in England. Substitute these at will when I call for stoneware clays.

Eastern Canada

In Eastern Canada a great many ceramic materials are imported from the United States and England, so the materials I call for in my recipes are generally available. There are, however, Canadian equivalents for some of the imported clays that Canadian ceramists may wish to use.

Western Canada

Ceramists in Western Canada often use materials in their glazes that are widely distributed throughout North America. Their clay bodies, however, often have western Canadian sources. The glaze recipes listed in Chapter 6 should work well with these clay bodies.

TRADE NAMES FOR GENERIC MATERIALS IN MY RECIPES

Ball clay—Old Mine No. 4

Boron frit—Ferro Frit #3124

High-impurity clay—Barnard Clay

High-iron clay—Cedar Heights Redart

Kaolin for clay bodies—Grolleg. Kaolin for glazes—EPK

Potash feldspar—Custer Feldspar

Soda feldspar—F4 Feldspar

Soda frit—Ferro Frit #3110

Stoneware clay—Cedar Heights Goldart

Zirconium opacifier—Zircopax

APPENDIX B: SAFE PRACTICES FOR THE CERAMIST

Every ceramist needs to be aware of the danger some of our materials pose to both ourselves and those who eat or drink from our pieces. Some materials are toxic and some are nontoxic but irritating and potentially dangerous.

TOXIC MATERIALS

Barium carbonate

All cadmium compounds

All chrome and chromate compounds

All lead compounds

Lithium carbonate

Manganese dioxide (powdered)

Nickel compounds

Vanadium pentoxide

It is especially important for ceramists working in oxidation to be aware of these problems because many of these materials formerly were used by ceramists working in the oxidation fire. Barium works well in both oxidation and reduction, but the rich, silky mat barium glazes with strong alkaline color were at one time a prominent feature of the oxidation fire. Both cadmium and chrome were most often used to produce rich color in the low-temperature oxidation fire. Lead has always been associated with the oxidation atmosphere; in reduction, it bubbles and blisters.

Lead frits, lithium feldspars, and stains containing vanadium and chrome contain toxic elements or strong irritants, but when they are combined with silica and alumina to create compounds (frits, feldspars, or stains), they are fairly safe to use. However, some highly acidic or alkaline foods may release these toxic elements. Therefore, even these safer compounds should never be used in glazes that might contact food.

TOXIC MATERIALS AND APPROPRIATE SUBSTITUTES

While no material can substitute in every way for another, the following material has been written as a guide for effective substitutions.

Barium Carbonate. Titanium dioxide, tin oxide, or zirconium opacifiers can serve as substitutes for barium carbonate. Use titanium dioxide and tin oxide in amounts of 7 to 20% and zirconium opacifiers in amounts of 20 to 30%. Additions in these percentages will encourage soft, mat surfaces with a rich sheen somewhat reminiscent of barium's mat effects.

Chrome and Chromate Compounds. Copper oxide or carbonate will serve as a partial substitute for greens derived from chrome. There are no real substitutes for pinks and crimsons derived from chrome. The brilliant fire-engine red and oranges derived from chrome/lead combinations are especially dangerous, and many ceramists would rather not use them. Unfortunately, there are no substitutes for these colors either.

Lead Compounds. Boron and sodium are fine melters and are useful substitutes for materials which contain lead.

Lithium Carbonate. Spodumene (a lithium-containing feldspar) is much less toxic than lithium carbonate and can serve as a useful substitute for it. If you would rather avoid lithium altogether, boron-containing compounds (boron frits and Gerstley borate) are the closest to lithium in their melting power. Small percentages of titanium (2–3%) are closest to lithium in their visual texture.

Manganese Dioxide (powdered). Black iron oxide is a fairly close substitute for powdered manganese dioxide.

Nickel Carbonate. There are no substitutes for this material.

Vanadium Pentoxide or Vanadium Stains. Titanium yellow stain is an excellent substitute.

OTHER SAFETY PROBLEMS

Many other safety problems affect only the ceramist, not the ultimate consumer. These include problems with dusts, grinding machinery, and kilns.

Dusts

Over a period of years, the dry materials ceramists use every day can cause respiratory damage and place many ceramists in real jeopardy. While all ceramists must learn to control the amount of ceramic dust that they inhale, some ceramists are particularly at risk. Those who should be most careful either have a disposition to respiratory problems or are heavy smokers. The elimination of smoking among ceramists would be the most important step in eliminating work-related health problems.

Respiratory Irritants

Bone ash

Clay

Cobalt colorants

All copper compounds

Feldspars

Gerstley borate (calcium, sodium borate)

Ground silica (flint)

Talc (calcium, magnesium silicate)

Wollastonite (calcium silicate)

Wood ash

Zinc oxide

Zirconium compounds

Safety When Making Clay or Glazes

Clay body and glaze making can be quite dangerous. The dry powders needed to make clay bodies and glazes are dusty, and these dusts can settle in the lungs. The work room should be well ventilated and dust should not be allowed to accumulate. Mop the studio frequently. Always wear an approved respirator. You may also wish to purchase disposable outer garments (see below).

SAFETY EQUIPMENT

Respirators

Some respirators purify the air of dusts, while others handle both dusts and fumes. In an ideal world we would not create dangerous dusts and fumes. In a slightly less ideal world we would be able to filter completely all impurities in the air and no one would be threatened by toxic dusts or fumes. Since the world is not ideal, we must filter dusts by wearing a face mask. While such protection is uncomfortable and inconvenient, it is quite efficient when used correctly.

Respirators fit over the nose and mouth and contain filters that allow oxygen to pass through but halt dusts and fumes. Disposable respirators can be used once or twice and then discarded. Although they are comparatively easy to wear, disposable masks are not efficient enough to be useful to the ceramist.

Some respirators are composed of a reusable facepiece and disposable filter cartridges. The sophisticated multilayer filters will filter extremely fine dusts, including ceramic dusts. These respirators are modular in design. The body of the mask (the facepiece) is made from a rubber-like material that seals out dust and fumes; disposable filtering cartridges are attached to this facepiece.

No one cartridge can be designed to deal with all of the problems that require a dust mask. Most manufacturers of respirators make a whole line of cartridges, each designed for a specific job. Some of these cartridges are so complex that they cost more than the facepiece: this should not surprise us as they are the real working part of the mask. Ceramists need cartridges that are meant to filter extremely fine dusts; occasionally we may also need the extra protection of filters to protect us from fumes (especially important during the kiln firing).

When to Replace the Filtering Cartridges

Ceramists often work in an environment in which the dust or fume level is not fully understood. It is therefore difficult to know when to change the filters on a respirator. If you sense irritation or experience an unpleasant smell or taste, change the filters immediately. Sometimes, however, there is no signal that can alert us that it is time to change the filters. Many ceramists place a mark on the filters for every hour the mask is worn and after so many hours (perhaps ten or twenty) exchange the old filters for new ones. This commonsense strategy is perhaps as useful as any. Always wash the facepiece when changing the filters.

Disposable Safety Garments

Disposable safety garments, made from a paper-like material, offer the ceramist good protection and they are inexpensive. They are especially useful to the ceramist working in dusty environments and are especially useful when preparing wood-ash glazes (see page 70). These garments are intended for disposal after a few wearings.

PROCEDURES FOR SAFELY PREPARING AND APPLYING GLAZES

When working with dry materials, the ceramist should wear a NIOSH (U.S.A.) or Factory Inspectorate (G.B.) approved dust respirator. When working with highly alkaline materials (such as wood ash), it is a good idea to wear special protective clothing (including headgear); paper safety suits are useful for this purpose.

Add water to dry materials as soon as possible. Never sieve dry mixtures; this can be extremely dusty. Sieving a wet mixture is far quicker and safer.

Most methods of glaze application are not particularly dangerous. Spraying, however, can be quite hazardous. Always wear a mask while spraying and spray into a well-vented spray booth.

BENCH GRINDERS

Ceramists find a great many uses for bench grinders; they are especially useful for grinding glaze off the bottom of a piece. Unfortunately, bench grinders can be dangerous. Flying ceramic chips can cause cuts or eye damage, and the rapidly turning grinding wheel can catch articles of clothing or hair and pull the ceramist toward the machine. When using the grinder, always wear a protective face shield, tie back long hair, and remove clothing that could become entangled in the grinding wheel.

PROCEDURES FOR SAFE KILN FIRING

Electric kilns carry heavy current loads, so it is crucial that the connections to electrical sources be installed carefully and professionally.

Ventilating dangerous gases produced during firing is a real problem for the ceramist using the electric kiln. Kilns should be placed in a separate room. Indoor kilns should be fitted with an efficient exhaust system that vents to the outside. Electric kilns may be fitted with an under-kiln or overhead hood. The under-kiln ventilation system seems to be very efficient for venting top-loading kilns. In this system a small hole is placed in the floor of the kiln and an exhaust fan draws the spent gases from this opening. These are vented to the outdoors.

Viewing the Kiln Interior During Firing

Most ceramists fire with cones (see page 4), and it is often necessary to look into the incandescent firing chamber to check the position of the cone. Doing this can cause eye damage. The ceramist should wear "tuned" safety glasses when looking into the kiln chamber during the latter part of the firing. Tuned glasses can be obtained from a safety supply house; the supplier will need to know the temperature you fire to in order to sell you glasses of the appropriate shade. Dr. Michael McCann in his book *Artist Beware* recommends welders glasses with the designation 2–2.5. These glasses are a great boon and are quite inexpensive. In addition to protecting the eyes, they make it easier to see the cone.

INDEX TO ARTISTS

Page references in *italic* refer to photographs

SUBJECT INDEX

Page references in *italic* refer to illustrations